TRACING YOUR
CRIMINAL ANCESTORS

D0770526

FAMILY HISTORY FROM PEN & SWORD

Tracing Your Yorkshire Ancestors
Rachel Bellerby

Tracing Your Royal Marine Ancestors
Richard Brooks and Matthew Little

Tracing Your Army Ancestors
Simon Fowler

A Guide to Military History on the Internet
Simon Fowler

Tracing Your Northern Ancestors
Keith Gregson

Tracing Your Irish Ancestors
Ian Maxwell

Tracing Your Air Force Ancestors
Phil Tomaselli

Tracing Your Jewish Ancestors
Rosemary Wenzerul

Tracing Your Textile Ancestors
Vivien Teasdale

Tracing Your Police Ancestors
Stephen Wade

TRACING YOUR
CRIMINAL ANCESTORS

STEPHEN WADE

Pen & Sword
FAMILY HISTORY

First published in Great Britain in 2009 by
PEN & SWORD FAMILY HISTORY
an imprint of
Pen & Sword Books Ltd
47 Church Street
Barnsley
South Yorkshire
S70 2AS

Copyright © Stephen Wade, 2009

ISBN 978 1 84884 057 7

Printed and bound in England by
CPI UK

Pen & Sword Books Ltd incorporates the Imprints of
Pen & Sword Aviation, Pen & Sword Family History, Pen & Sword Maritime,
Pen & Sword Military, Wharncliffe Local History, Pen & Sword Select,
Pen & Sword Military Classics, Leo Cooper, Remember When,
Seaforth Publishing and Frontline Publishing

For a complete list of Pen & Sword titles please contact
PEN & SWORD BOOKS LIMITED
47 Church Street, Barnsley, South Yorkshire, S70 2AS, England
E-mail: enquiries@pen-and-sword.co.uk
www.pen-and-sword.co.uk

CONTENTS

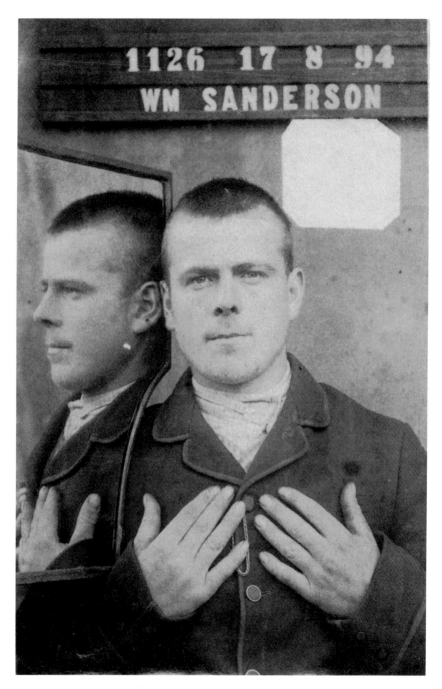

William Sanderson, a habitual offender – the record being mainly petty theft and fraud. East Riding of Yorkshire Archives

INTRODUCTION

'CRIMINAL' – A SURVEY OF THE WORD IN SOURCES

To trace criminal ancestors is to face the complex task of making sense of how the words 'crime' and 'criminal' have been placed within the law of England over the centuries. A criminal is an offender who breaks the criminal law, but the process of trial and sentencing that subsequently happens is something that may involve a much wider range of locations and institutions than the courts of criminal law. When the first circuits of the judges were established, two judges would be in transit, one for the criminal and one for the civil courts. But for the modern historian, the ancestor may not be found in the court labelled 'criminal' because some offences were tried elsewhere.

Also, definitions of what is criminal and what is not have shifted over time according to political ideologies, changing moral structures and the adaptations of criminal law as society changed. A simple example would be to refer to the one criminal ancestor in my own family (there may be others as yet undiscovered). This was an uncle who took his own life, and when he did so, in 1958, suicide was a criminal offence. Had he taken his life two years later he would not have been a criminal.

What was seen as behaviour so heinous that the offender had to be outlawed in c.1200 may well have been something rated much less terrible a century later. In particular periods in the past, larger political factors have been an influence on crime and punishment. A researcher studying assize rolls from the King's Bench and the circuit in 1300 would be amazed to see how many truly awful offences were punished with fines, and one reason for this was that the King needed cash, and so fines were a simple and uncomplicated source of revenue.

A clear example of how this affects research into family history is the case of debtors. One's ancestor may indeed have spent time in a prison – but as a debtor, not as anyone who was a danger to society. Equally, the case of mental illness is one that will affect research: an asylum would be a destination for a convict, rather than a prison or a transportation vessel, and so enquiries may often move laterally into areas of medicine and social health, complementing the study of criminal records per se.

A SUMMARY OF HISTORICAL CRIME RESEARCH

In 1883, at Durham assizes, Jane Clark was indicted for unlawfully exposing the dead body of a child in a public highway. This was a common law misdemeanour and she was indicted for a nuisance. As Elijah Scott of West Hartlepool was going from work at eight in the morning, he found the dead body of a child on the foot pavement near his back door. The child was naked and mutilated.

What emerged was that Jane Clark, the mother, had been indicted for child murder but this indictment had failed; for the second indictment, the jury had to be convinced that the body had been placed there, and by the mother. Jane was found guilty and given six months in gaol, but without hard labour.

If Jane Clark had been one of your ancestors, the paper trail relating to her would have led you to the magistrates' court, then to quarter sessions, and finally to the reports know as crown cases reserved (published in volume form). You would also need to have some idea what the legal vocabulary meant: words such as misdemeanour and

Bow Street magistrates' court, a typical metropolitan magistrate's court.
Author's collection

indictable. Such a task is worth the effort because under the official texts there is a powerful human tale. Jane Clark needed all kinds of help, and today she would have had that easily available. In 1883 there was no safety net for extreme poverty except for the workhouse, for working-class people. Jane Clark was clearly mentally ill, and had most likely endured post-natal depression or psychosis. But her story ends with a prison sentence, and her dead child becomes a 'public nuisance'.

For these reasons, there are some sensible first steps to make before the actual historical research begins:

• Have a dictionary of law in order to check on terminology.
• Read some court reports merely to see what process at trial happened.
• Have a grasp of the basic language of sentencing and charging.
• Understand what courts existed and for what purposes.

These will all be included in the first two sections of this book, before the first chapter of topics and case studies.

The simplified process of finding a criminal ancestor can be seen in this sequence:

1 A family ancestor is not present in the usual records and so may have been in prison. A search of county registers for prisons will establish his or her destiny.
2 There will then be documents called calendars of prisoners and these will list offences, locations and magistrates involved.
3 The case may have gone to court and so the next step is to access court records. These may be in any one of a large number of courts, but the most likely places to look are in reports of quarter sessions, petty sessions, assizes, the Old Bailey or, for crimes not in the main system, the Palatinate courts or in Great Sessions of Wales. The areas known as the Palatinates were the counties of Cheshire, Durham and Lancashire. These had their own courts, up until 1830 for Cheshire and 1876 for Durham and Lancashire. If your ancestor's crime was dealt with by the mainstream criminal justice system then the name and details will be in these locations.
4 Prison records should then be found, and these existed in a variety of forms (see Chapter 10).

With the preceding information, a fair amount of biography has been ascertained. To build on that, there are hundreds of different documents scattered in all kinds of places that will be useful, but newspaper reports are a good starting point.

Transportation may have been the destination, because 160,000 people were transported to Australia between 1787 and 1867. Fortunately, there are a number of helpful sources in this context.

If your ancestor was not dealt with in the main system, then other courts need to be accessed. The nature of the offence is your best guide here because offences that were clearly relevant to moral issues or to marital or behavioural aspects relating to church matters were handled in ecclesiastical courts.

The internet search may be a profitable starting point of course because researchers in family history societies may well have made some progress with minor sources and these will emerge in all kinds of contexts on the Internet.

Crime research in history may also involve earlier periods. The above list relates mainly to criminal activity between c.1700 and the present. But for people before this, even reaching back to the medieval period, there are sources relating to all kinds of courts and many of these are now in print or on CD. A visit to a university library can also be useful in accessing these kinds of records.

Before we look at the courts through history, here is a checklist of essential terminology. Without an understanding of these, the first steps with texts will be much harder.

Offences
Summary and indictable
A summary offence may be tried by a magistrate only, whereas an indictable offence has to be tried before a jury. This relates also to the definitions of felony and misdemeanour: a felony, until the Criminal Law Act of 1967 was a serious offence, and before 1870, it meant that the convict would forfeit all lands and chattels, and often being sentenced to death as well. A misdemeanour was a less extreme offence, usually tried summarily. In the records and texts relating to your ancestor, these words will occur.

Documents
Order Books
From 1629 to 1749 these were draft orders and memoranda books,

LINCOLNSHIRE,   LINDSEY TO WIT.

CALENDAR OF   PRISONERS

AT KIRTON OCTOBER SESSIONS,
ON FRIDAY THE 17TH DAY OF OCTOBER, 1851.

The letter *N.* denotes the prisoner cannot read or write.—*Imp.* read, or read or write imperfectly.—*Well,* read or write well.—*Sup.* superior education.
—The letter *h. l.* hard labour.—The asterisk (*) the number of times the prisoner has been committed.—
The parallel lines(‖) those who have been convicted of felony.

READ AND WRITE.	NAMES.	WHEN COMMITTED.	OFFENCES.	COMMITTING MAGISTRATES.	SENTENCES.
Imp	1 James Riley	16 July 7th	Stealing at Gainsborough, one Silver Watch, the property of James Whiley.	Rev. G. Hutton	
N	2 William Andrews	23 July 13th	Stealing at Gainsborough, three pieces of Silver coin called Shillings, two pieces of Copper coins called Pennys, one other piece of Copper coin called a Halfpenny, and one Crown, the property of Elizabeth Wilson.	Rev. C. W. Hudson	
N	3 Mary Ann Andrews				
Imp	4 John Drury*	28 July 17th	Stealing at Burrow, one Bacon Ham, a quantity of threshed Wheat, and a Calico Bag, the property of John Robinson.	S. Wormald, Esq.	
N	5 James Mew*?	24 July 22nd	Stealing at Barton, two pieces of Gold coin called Sovereigns, and seven pieces of Silver coin called Shillings, the property of James Maw, senior.	G. C. Uppleby, Esq.	
Imp	6 Elizabeth Thompson	60 July 24th	Uttering at Haxey, one Brass Pan, the pro-perty of false & counterfeit coin resembling a Crown piece, and having other pieces of false and counterfeit Coin in her possession, well-knowing them to be false and counterfeit.	H. B. Smith, Esq.	
Imp	7 John Thomas	26 Aug.	Stealing at Haxey, one Brass Pan, the pro-perty of Joseph Beacroft.	Ven. Archden. Stonehouse	
Imp	8 Martha Brown, otherwise Martha Eden	37 Aug. 4th	Stealing at Thonock, twelve yards of Carpet, the property of Henry Bacon Hickman, Esq.	H. B. Smith, Esq.	
Imp	9 William Newton	20 Aug. 16th	Stealing at Hibbaldstow, one Waistcoat, one Shirt, and other articles, the property of Thomas Hancox.	Sir J. Nelthorpe, Bart.	
Imp	10 Valentine Geddins	25 Sept. 1st	Stealing at Willingham, two Heifers, the pro-perty of John Hopkinson.	W. Hutton, Esq.	
Imp	11 William Hill	25 Sept. 1st	Receiving at Willingham, the above Heifers, well-knowing them to have been Stolen, the property of John Hopkinson.	W. Hutton, Esq.	
Imp	12 Thomas Hill net?	60			
N	13 Andrew Hart	48 Sept. 9th	Stealing at Thornton, one Jacket, the pro-perty of Charles Kirman.	W. D. Field, Esq.	
Imp	14 Elizabeth Cummins	27 Sept. 19th	Stealing at Gainsborough, two pair of Stays, five Blankets, one Woollen Scarf, and other articles, the property of John Moore.	Rev. J. T. Huntley Rev. J. Stockdale	
Imp	15 John Gray	.. Sept. 25th	Stealing at Stamford, one Cotton Shirt, the property of Matthew Sharman.	Rev. J. T. Huntley	
Imp	16 James Smith	28 Oct. 9th	Stealing at South Ferriby, one Silk Handker-chief, the property of George Drury.	G. C. Uppleby, Esq.	
N	17 John Uffindale	29 Oct. 13th	Stealing at Roxand, two tame Rabbits, the property of George Crowcroft; also stealing at Crowle, one Turkey, the property of John Bmayse; and further charged with stealing at Roxand, one Rabbit, the proper-ty of Richard Thornton.	G. S. Lister, Esq. Rev. J. Dobson T. H. Lister, Esq.	
N	18 Henry Stainforth	30 Oct. 13th	Stealing at Roxand, one tame Rabbit, the pro-perty of Richard Thornton; also stealing at Roxand, one tame Rabbit, the property of George Crowcroft.	G. S. Lister, Esq. Rev. J. Dobson T. H. Lister, Esq.	
Imp	19 Maonty Daniel	23 Oct. 14th	At Caistor, did attempt feloniously and bur-glariously to break and enter the Dwelling-house of William Pybus.	Rev. J. T. Hales Tooke	

A calendar of prisoners, listing the basic details of offence and trial.
Lincolnshire Archives

and after 1750 there were no sessions rolls, which had been the main records since the medieval period.

Calendars of prisoners

These are lists of the prisoners held before trial, and they provide plenty of information, including the crime, by whom the prisoner was committed into custody, and the date of the warrant for the arrest.

Indictment rolls

An indictment is a formal statement of a charge. Rolls give the names of offenders, with details of offences and the dates of conviction.

Recognizance books

This is a surety or a bond, given before an official, existing to secure a performance by the person stated. The document will provide names and statements relating to the accused persons.

The Sessions House, Beverley. The Georgian façade is typical of so many similar courts. The author

Quarter sessions rolls and petitions

Quarter sessions were held in the circuits of the land, four times a year; these had been meetings of magistrates since 1361, though there had been justices of the peace since the Statute of Winchester in 1285. The rolls were the final records of the court. Petitions provide reference about people who appeared at the courts. Some record offices may have these names compiled into an index.

Writs

Originally, a writ was how an action in the common law started its course through the legal system, and a writ was also a document in the sovereign's name and under the seal of the crown commanding a person not to do a particular act.

THE COURTS IN HISTORY

In the 1850s, Charles Dickens edited a journal called *Household Narrative*; in this publication we find summary reports under the heading 'Law and Crime' and a glance at the 1854 collected volumes has reports from these courts: a court-martial; Lincolnshire Assizes; the London Guildhall; Bow Street Magistrates' Court; Marlborough Street Police Court; a coroner's inquest at Hunslet, Leeds, and the Court of Queen's Bench sitting in Dublin. Criminal ancestors were present in all these locations, with crimes ranging from 'stealing a bit of velvet riband' to a case of 'wilful murder against Joseph Baines' who was charged with killing his wife. Such is the proliferation of courts and trials in British history and the family historian needs to find a way through this labyrinth.

For the criminal records, the main courts you will be concerned with are petty sessions, quarter sessions and assizes. From 1971 the assizes were replaced by crown courts.

Assizes

These were held from the thirteenth century until 1971. The system had its origins in which two judges would hold the sovereign's court twice a year. These tried criminal cases and civil. From 1550 records provide details of such offences as homicide, infanticide and major theft. Before 1733 assize records are in Latin and the main records are indictments (statements of charges); depositions (written evidences) and gaol books or minutes (lists of accused persons and summaries of cases heard). If there are no assize records surviving, then there are sheriffs' assize vouchers, located at THA E389 and also, for writs, the King's Bench records.

The *Gentleman's Magazine* published details of the assize circuits, such as this entry from the 1819 issue: 'Spring Circuits, 1819: Norfolk, Lord Chief Justice Abbott and baron Graham: Aylesbury, March 4, Bedford March 10, Huntingdon March 13, Thetford March 20, Bury St Edmund's March 26.'

Quarter Sessions

These were where the justices of the peace sat in judgement, from their creation in 1285. By the eighteenth century these 'bench' meetings had a massive work load.

Petty Sessions

These were summary courts, dealing with all kinds of minor matters, normally with two magistrates sitting. From 1828, quarter sessions

'A court of petty sessions' in Ireland. Author's collection

were empowered to form county petty sessions. Increasingly in the Victorian period, police courts took over the handling of everyday criminal proceedings. The simplest way to understand what these were and how they worked is to search in the Times Digital Archive for such as 'Hull Police Court' and study some examples.

For criminal proceedings this was the structure:
Magistrates/summary courts/petty sessions – assizes – appeal courts (limited and for the wealthy) – High Court of Justice – Court of Criminal Appeal (for all since 1907) – House of Lords. Notice that appeal courts are added here to the normal main three courts. If your ancestor committed a serious crime, the appeal may have gone to the very top, as in rare cases of condemned convicts who appealed for a respite (a pardon or commutation of sentence).

In addition to these, other courts relevant to your research will be (all will occur in the following case studies):

Coroners' courts
The first hearing for responses to deaths, suspicious or otherwise. These were often held in public houses.

Courts martial
A military court, where your criminal ancestor may have had his case heard, rather than in a criminal court.

Church courts
These have various names and have unusual jurisdiction, such as the Court of Arches, whose records are at Lambeth Palace. But church Consistory courts would often sit in cathedrals and hear cases within the Bishop's jurisdiction.

OFFICIALS IN THE CRIMINAL JUSTICE SYSTEM
It is also worthwhile to be aware of the functions of various offices within the system. The main ones are as follows:

Coroner
Under the Normans, he was 'the keeper of the pleas of the crown' and so was a 'crowner'. The coroner sits at inquests and also used to define what deodands (payments to the crown) would be paid.

Justice of the Peace
An act of 1327 stated that a person had to be appointed in each county to be responsible for keeping the peace of the sovereign. The Justices of the Peace Act in 1361 defined them as justices, and they were usually powerful locals such as Lords of the Manor.

Lord-Lieutenant
He was originally a military householder, but then, since the sixteenth century, he has been the representative of the sovereign in the county at the highest level. He was also responsible for keeping the county records, and was the person who organised militia and communal defence in emergency.

Parish Constable
At first he was appointed by the court leet of the manor (see next section). He had to supervise, watch and ward, the first real system of

Lord Hewart, Lord Chief Justice 1922-40.
He heard many high-profile cases.
Author's collection

community vigilance, but he also had several other duties, including impounding stray animals and supervise beggars and vagrants.

Sheriff
This was originally a 'shire reeve' – the deputy of the crown. He was the main organiser of the courts before the justices appeared, and he ran the militia.

THE PROCESS OF RESEARCH
A tried and tested method of making your research develop into far more than merely facts from the archives is to make notes as you progress, and follow the lateral leads into other material. For instance, a court report in which the ancestor figured will help in understanding the nature of a crime but also it will have (a) legal terms (b) explanations of how the legal process worked and (c) clues about other paper records generated or about what happened after the sentence or acquittal. A typical case would be a violent crime in which there was a question of diminished responsibility; another example might be a trial before the 1820s when there were over 200

capital offences. The process might work like this, in an imaginary case of c.1820:

- The trial takes place and we learn of the social circumstances.
- There is a sentence given.
- Then some prison records.
- But many sentences were commuted, so Home Office papers could be consulted.
- A death sentence would often become commuted to transportation, so these records are generated.

THE NATIONAL ARCHIVES (TNA)

Go to the main website and in the search window put 'criminal records.'

In recent years The National Archives have created extremely useful research guides, on their website, to most major aspects of criminal history. The main categories are:

(1) Home Office records: HO Divisions. For instance, there are coroners' records, remissions and pardons, entry books of criminals, registers of criminals, convict records, warrant books of criminals and calendars of prisoners here.

(2) Prison records: these cover a wide variety of sources, including medical journals, gaolers' returns, calendars of indictments, registers of prison hulks, transportation records, criminal entry books, petitions, registers of county prisons, warrant books and judges' reports. These are dealt with fully in Chapter 10.

(3) Assize records: From 1559 these deal with serious crime, including highway robbery, rape, assault, forgery and witchcraft. An indispensable feature of this is a key for criminal trials by county, so that for example, we have lists of trial records for each county and the list tells the reader what is available under the groupings of:

Crown and gaol books
Indictments
Depositions
Other materials

LOCAL RECORD OFFICES

The Access to Archives facility (known as A2A) on The National Archives website provides listings of holdings at county record offices, but a visit will be necessary to see the materials. In Lincolnshire Archives, for example, there are printed assize calendars covering the years 1771 to 1971. Most assize records are at The National Archives, but at Lincoln there are materials under three categories: calendars of prisoners, calendars of sentences and gaol delivery calendars. The basis of the circuit assize system was called Oyez and terminer which means to 'hear and determine' and also the task of gaol delivery. In other words, the travelling justices' main tasks were to hear cases, determine sentences and clear the gaols in so doing of course. Twice a year this would happen, so prisoners on remand without bail could spend a long time in unpleasant gaols waiting for their Lordships.

The relevant record office for your ancestor will have similar documents, and in the case of Lincoln, there are helpful lists relating to offprints giving information (from newspapers and from gaol records) on criminals. The sources most often met with, as mentioned above, contain these details:

Calendars of prisoners – name, crime, age, literacy, occupation, place of residence and date of committal.
Calendars of sentences – The same as the above, but with sentences recorded.
Gaol delivery calendars – names, sentences and descriptions of crimes. These were printed after the assize hearings.

It also has to be mentioned that local record offices will have earlier materials from medieval and early modern times, such as manorial rolls and information on court leets.

INTERNET RESOURCES
The numbers of internet sources and resources from tracing criminal ancestry are increasing rapidly. With some payment, access to and use of many sites will speed up some of the process of discovery. However, arguably the most fruitful first steps are in trying the well-established organisations, and what is found at The National Archives will almost always lead to other sources. There is a full account of these resources in my bibliography section, but at the preliminary stage it should be mentioned here that these online resources are worth looking at immediately, as the researcher sets out

the scope of the enquiry:
Access to Archives (A2A) www.nationalarchives.go.uk/a2a
Archives Hub www.archiveshub.ac.uk
British Library Online Newspaper Archive www.uk.Olivesoftware.com
National Archives of Ireland www.nationalarchives.ie
National Archives of Scotland www.nas.go.uk
National Library of Wales www.llgc.org.uk
Newgate Calendar www.exclassics.com/newgate/ngintro/htm
Old Bailey Proceedings www.oldbaileyonline.org

Also worth looking at now, at the point of departure, are the resources online provided by national newspapers and by an organisation called Black Sheep Index.

The Times Digital Archive and the Guardian Digital Archive can be very useful of course, for searching terms such as courts and names once the researcher knows the dates of the family member's life or career. The Black Sheep Index provides lists of newspaper items by name and date and, for a small fee, it is possible to order the actual source document. There is a section on the site devoted to 'Lags and Screws' and it is possible to search for names: all items come from press reports.

A SURVEY OF 'SMALL BUSINESS': SUMMARY COURTS AND COURT LEETS

RECORDS IN COURTS FOR SUMMARY OFFENCES

Magistrates did not send very many cases on to quarter sessions; throughout the centuries, small misdemeanours were dealt with quickly and efficiently. As Peter King has written in his study of these courts: 'In almost every county there were also many magistrates who heard individual cases alone in their homes' and he notes that, 'an increasing number of both administrative and legal functions were passed down to them by the legislature...' (see Bibliography).

We can have a glimpse at this kind of record if we look at *The Justicing Notebook of Edmund Tew*, Rector of Bolden, published by the Surtees Society. In his journal we find entries such as these:

1763 November 15th. Granted general warrant against Isabel Reed of Shields, fruiterer, for defrauding... Of ditto widow a pair of shoes. Agreed.

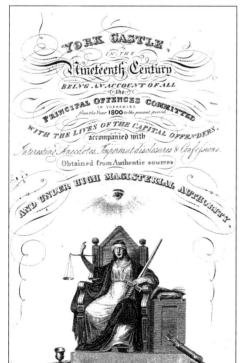

22nd Granted a search warrant against George Turner of Jarrow, farmer, for concealing timber in his outhouse of Robert Waynman of North Shields. Agreed.

York Castle, an early Victorian crime chronicle. Author's collection

For various areas of the North East and the North West of England, the publications of the Chetham Society and the Surtees Society provide a great deal of detail of offenders in those areas in the Early Modern period, and in fact, the court leet records of Manchester for the sixteenth century give a very substantial account of such legal practices. A court leet was a type of summary court, probably coming from the Old English verb *gelethian*, to assemble together. Manchester ancestors who transgressed even in these very minor ways can be located in the records and indexes. For instance, at the court held on 15 April, 1579:

> William Linley shall from the old ancient quickwood standing at the east end of his garden hedge to the green quickwood beneath the apple-tree to the church-yard, set his hedge straight...

And in 1574:

> If any alehouse keeper man or woman be found drunken, in their own house or elsewhere, he or she shall be punished by imprisonment one night and from thenceforth be discharged from ale-house keeping.

These sources show just what a huge amount of everyday law was handled by the magistrates and the justices presiding at leets and petty sessions. The topics coming before the sessions could be anything from petty theft to homicide, but much of the time was taken up with sorting out people from other parishes who had come into another parish, or with lack of payment to constables. Often it was a matter of debating issues such as who should repair a certain bridge or what should be done with a deserter.

The Bibliography has more information on these lesser-known sources. With every day that passes, more and more of these texts are made available, and are often found in university libraries as well as in local archives.

DEBTORS, DESERTERS AND DRUNKS
Debtors
Debt cases in history will involve access to and scrutiny of civil court records. Obviously, this misfortune is linked to credit and to

individuals or families living beyond their means. General newspapers and trade papers list debtors and bankrupts. These unfortunate people found themselves living in awful gaols and houses of correction, and the prison reformer, John Howard, estimated that in 1779 there were 2,000 debtors in the gaols.

The simplest way to grasp the lives and destinations of debtors is to look at the main gaols in London in the eighteenth century: the Fleet, the Marshalsea, Whitecross Street and the Fleet. The defining characteristic of these places was that they were businesses. For instance, the house of correction at Northallerton, the oldest prison still in the Prison Service Establishment, began in the 1780s with a division of debtors and prisoners on sentence or on remand. Vagrants, debtors and ruffians were together (male) but the women were kept in separate accommodation. It was essentially a factory: all work was logged in a daily labour book, giving the amount of work done, and these figures were then transferred into quarterly books, with all costs monitored.

By 1520 there were 180 offences that were punishable by a prison term. Debt actions figured in this as results of civil actions, the result of one citizen prosecuting another for debt, and then prison followed, not as a punishment but to make sure that the debtor was under supervision until such time as he could gather some funds and pay the debt. In the Fleet, in the 1770s, there were 242 debtors, and they lived there with their families. In *Little Dorrit*, Dickens presents a picture of life in the Marshalsea, the prison where his father, John, had been imprisoned for debt.

Cases of debts had been handled at the Court of Requests through the centuries until the Small Debts Bill of 1845 when county courts were established. As Charles Nicholl has recently shown in his book, *The Lodger*, Shakespeare was involved in a claim at this court – giving evidence on 11 May 1612 in the lawsuit Belott v Mountjoy. Nicholl provides an interesting sidelight on historical research when he notes that the first historian of the case had to work with uncalendared bundles of papers at the Court of Requests archives in 1909.

There was a report on the Great Yarmouth bridewell in 1818 that pointed out the fate of debtors at that time:

The apartments for the debtors are mostly above stairs and are

What an eighteenth century prison wing looked like. The author

in a tolerably Good state. There are about nine beds for master debtors and three for common Debtors: but in one room appropriated to the latter class, 21 feet by 12 eight

Or ten have slept at one time. Debtors from the Court of Requests have been Sent in contiguous thereto... I was told hat the prisoners were kept shut up In their cells all the day as well as during the night...

The Small Debts Bill of 1845 brought in the very sensible measure of securing the payment of judgement debts not exceeding £20. It enabled a creditor to apply to any court for the recovery of the debt and made county courts and any other court for the recovery of small debts a part of the system.

Deserters

In the issue of the *Police Gazette* for 11 November 1829, there is a double-page containing, 'A List and Description of Deserters from His Majesty's Service' with entries such as:

ROYAL MARINES

Zachariah Mott Chatham Division Ridgmont Parish Suffolk blacksmith age 28

He was 5 feet 7 inches, with grey eyes and dark hair; was 'supposed to have gone in to Essex to work at the harvest' and had been 'last seen in Portsmouth'. This is a great deal of detailed information about the man.

Even in the *Newcastle Courant* for May 1803 we have this notice:

Deserted from His Majesty's Fifth regiment of Dragoon Guards, in the Morning of the second inst., aged 21 yrs. 6 ft high, dark complexion, Black hair, grey eyes, heavy limbs, walks awkwardly, was from Yorkshire And is by trade a woolcomber...

ROBERT BARKER

There was a reward of twenty shillings for information leading to his arrest.

In the first century AD, when Tacitus was writing of these islands, he stated: 'Traitors and deserters they hang on trees; the cowardly fighter, the shirker of military service and those who have polluted their bodies by vice they plunge into a foul swamp with a hurdle put over them.' In more recent times, in the years up to the Victorian period, the most frequent result of desertion would be a court martial and a flogging. But of course, the subject covers not only mass desertions from the British forces in the war with Napoleon, but the deserters of the Great War. In the latter case, the research will encounter poignant statistics: there were 306 soldiers shot at dawn from British courts-martial: these included 25 Canadians, 22 Irishmen and 5 New-Zealanders. There are even disgusting and very moving photographic records of some of these shootings, such as that of a Belgian soldier, Alois Walput, aged just twenty-one, shot on a beach of the North Sea, tied to a pole.

But the Admiralty Courts in the eighteenth and nineteenth centuries are full of reports concerning deserters, and many of these are accessible online, using the Times Digital Archive. Of course, desertion was a massive problem, and it is not surprising, as so many recruits were criminals who had chosen the army rather than gaol in the eighteenth century for instance. Richard Holmes, the military historian, has written: 'Some soldiers made a career of deserting after taking the bounty, but the introduction of branding on the arm, head or chest with D for deserter or BC for bad character made it impossible for a man already convicted of desertion to re-enlist.' Pursuit of deserters was undertaken, as in 1762, when Corporal John Jones deserted from a regiment in Lichfield, and that was after he was sent to catch a deserter. A notice was issued with his description.

A trawl through the various magistrates' and police courts in the nineteenth century brings examples of the processes involved in the capture and prosecution of deserters. For instance, in Preston at the police court in January 1859, John Ashby who had been in the borough police force but then joined the 8th Hussars, deserted from that force and gave himself up. He said he had deserted five months earlier and his fate was to be 'Remanded to the house of correction, to await orders from the regimental authorities.'

Similarly, in Dublin, a deserter gave himself up in 1844. This was Robert Ahearne, and he was interrogated at the Henry Street police court. That source notes that he had enlisted in the 97th Regiment at Burr in 1838 and he had absconded in Limerick in 1840.

Drunks

If the skeleton in the cupboard was in court for drunkenness, then the story will almost certainly open up a great deal more about the narrative of the time and the social context. In other words, although the reasons why people take too much alcohol are many and commonly understood, there is also a strong link between drunkenness and the economic pressures of the time in question. This is why, in British history, the rise of industrialism and the growth of cities provides the backdrop to so many offences involving drink. The fondness for gin through the eighteenth century and Victorian period, along with the increasing number of beer shops, explain much of the related crime. It was not uncommon for working people to partake of a beer in the early morning, on their way to their work.

Even back in Elizabethan times, England had a reputation for unrestrained beer-drinking. In *Othello*, Shakespeare has Iago say that he learned a drinking song in England:

> I learned it in England, where indeed they are most potent in potting: Your Dane, your German and your swag-bellied Hollander – drink ho! – are nothing to your English. (II iii 71-74)

In the eighteenth century there was a massive consumption of gin – 'Madame Geneva' – and there is a staggering statistic of nineteen million gallons of that drink being consumed in 1742. Clearly, as working patterns changed with the enclosure of land and the drift into the new towns for factory work continued, problems with drink accelerated in all classes. A typical case was a hearing at the Westminster sessions in 1813 when a man called Hynde was indicted for assaulting one Philip Kirkman. The report has this account: 'The prosecutor stated that the defendant had been his porter and that he had parted with him for drunkenness and abusive behaviour. On being applied by him, on two several times, for a character, the prosecutor gave him the character he deserved.' Kirkman was abused and attacked by Hynde. He was found guilty and given a prison term of one month. That would be a very typical case throughout most of English history in police courts and summary courts.

From the mid-Victorian times, the growth of teetotal movements is noticeable, and campaigns to keep the working man from drink were apparent everywhere, but most notably in the industrial communities. It could be said that drink was the scourge of the Victorian age; in 1874, the *Leeds Mercury* reported that the women of Leeds had organised a petition to the magistrates, asking for the number of licensed premises to be reduced. On one

A local shaming punishment, the stocks, general punishments from petty sessions. Author's collection

Saturday in that year, someone had logged the number of visitors to just one public house and the number was 2,215 people, of which 237 had been children.

In 1908, the Licensing Bill set out to reduce the number of licensed premises, the first real attempt to do something about this huge social problem. Between 1860 and 1870 arrests for drunkenness had more than doubled. In only a half mile of the working-class area of Birmingham, there were a hundred drinking houses, and in Liverpool there were forty-six pubs in just a 200 yard radius. The first licensing acts had been passed in 1872, but it was the Peel Commission of 1896 that really began to change matters. The *Illustrated London News* for the autumn of 1908 had a feature on a State Inebriates' Reformatory in Aylesbury and the point made was that the inhabitants had a 'pleasant lot' there. A reading of the books published by the 'Police Court Missionaries' of the last years of the nineteenth century shows a very different picture: they have accounts of habitual drunkards being cared for by the active philanthropists who preceded the first probation officers, who did not appear until 1907.

A police magistrate in London wrote in *The North American Review* for 1897, referring to the Peel Commission, of an habitual drunkard (this was a legal definition of a particular type of offender):

> The most notorious of these was a woman called Jane Cakebread... She was a curious creature who never seemed to be in the least disconcerted at her frequent appearances in court. Tall, spare and strong, with a plain but rather pleasing countenance, she always appeared in the dock as neat as circumstances would permit... She seldom or never found fault with the constable who arrested her.

This gives an insight into the way in which offenders for drunkenness fitted in with the course of everyday policing. Police officers were not exempt from the perils of drink, either: a common occurrence in police punishment books is this type of note (from an archive of Hull City Police in 1868): 'Being drunk when coming off duty at 6 p.m.' On the other hand, instruction books for constables had the sentence: 'A constable should interfere and arrest any drunken or violent men who threaten the life of any person in his hearing or under his observation.'

Thomas Holmes, the 'police court missionary' and author. Author's collection

CONSTABLES, COMMUNITY AND PARISH

For many of these crimes related to drink, desertion and debt, a study of quarter-sessions records will add more substance to the legal contexts. For instance, without the need to spend time at the archives, it is possible to consult the publications of historical societies for this information. The Yorkshire Archaeological Society, for example, have published Quarter Sessions Records of the West Riding, and these gather together trial records held at various towns across that area. At the centre of this process were the constables, and if they did not keep up to their work, entries such as this tend to appear:

Whereas John Fowler and Samuel Walton, late constables of Halifax, have Not made any account of the money they received last year upon their Constable layes within the town of Halifax... ORDERED that they shall Account before Mr Nathaniel Waterhouse...

Most of the business of these sessions was concerned with petty theft, assault, receiving, causing a public nuisance, and in particular, business pertaining to vagrants, as this entry from 1638 when five men were in court: '... being sound in body and able to work... and being unable to give a reason by what means they gain their living, were found begging and bearing themselves as vagabonds against the King's peace...'

These types of records show the nature of local crime and the shaming punishments being given – such things as stocks, pillory and branding, or even public whippings.

RESEARCH PROCESS

Debtors

For bankrupts, records are held at The National Archives in record series B. There is a downloadable research guide also. The *London Gazette* listed debtors and bankrupts, and a trawl in the relevant years in The Times Digital Archive will bring lists of bankrupts – some being famous, such as the artist Thomas Rowlandson on two occasions. The *London Gazette* may be accessed online in some universities with an Athens system for students and researchers.

At TNA see the research guide on 'Bankrupts and Insolvent Debtors' (from 1710 to 1939).

Deserters

For army records there are extensive documents at The National Archives. For the deserters from the British army, there are the Returns of Deserters, from 1811 to 1852 and these are arranged by regiment and by date of desertion. There is here a record of the man and of his place of enlistment. For the years 1813 to 1848 there are also the Register of Commitments, showing the names of men caught or surrendered. The reference numbers for all these are 2934 and 2954.

In Records of Men Deserting from the British Army – Your Archives, will be found a full description such as where born/trade/age/size and complexion/ clothing/ place of desertion. There are also entry books giving more information on some men.

For more recent years, the main sources are at various places, including War Office (WO) series TS46/132; the Home Office HO 47 Judges' reports; the Law Officers' Department for merchant shipping; Metropolitan Police Officer of the Commissioner (arrest of absentees and deserters from women's services); Arrest of Army Deserters at

Metropolitan Police, Office of the Commissioner. There are also Deserter Bounty Certificates in W182. The guidance notes at the Archives state: 'It is likely that these parties were adept at spotting deserters posing as respectable labourers. The seized deserters... were committed to the local clinks to await the arrival of collecting parties from their regiments.' Logically, with such a wide span of time being covered here, the material available will vary considerably.

Drunkards

In magistrates' courts, police courts and in police records, as well as in newspapers and magazines, accounts of crime linked to drunkenness may be traced. If the dates are known, it will not take long to access an account of the offence and the hearing in local newspapers. Also useful are coroners' court records and the starting point for these is to check in *Coroners' Records in England and Wales* by Gibson and Rogers. The Royal Historical Society produces a massive bibliography of crime and law and that can lead to some useful sources. There is a free research guide to coroners' inquests at The National Archives. Often, particular historical groups or researchers will produce materials from coroners' courts.

Usefully, between 1752 and 1860, coroners had to file their inquests at the quarter sessions, so the material wanted may be in the quarter sessions records at the county record offices. The Access to Archives facility (A2A) will list the records available across the country. Access to more modern records may be more difficult, as records within the last thirty years may be opened only at the discretion of the coroner.

If the search is for material before 1752, stretching back to 1128, then the main details are that from 1487 to 1752 coroners had to send their returns to the assize judges and then these would be forwarded to the court of King's Bench, so in The National Archives, reference KB 11 and also KB 13 will find these, the latter being from the Western Circuit up to 1820. In the Middlesex indictments for 1675 to 1845 there are some coroners' reports, and more in KB 12, KB 13 and KB 140.

It must also be recalled here that the palatinate courts had their records separately held, so for Chester the coroners' records are at CHES18 for the years 1339-1850; at ASSI 66 for 1798-1891; for Lancaster they are at PL 26/285-295 and for Lancaster Duchy they are at DL 46 for 1817-1896.

Coroners' courts have their roots in the office of coroner,

established in the late 1100s. The first coroners appeared in 1194. It was their job to collect a murder fine in the early period and supervise the trial of serious crime. These prosecutions were called pleas of the crown. The basic function was explained in the late sixteenth century by Sir Thomas Smith: 'If any man, woman or child be violently slain, the murderer not known, no man ought or dare bury the body before the coroner hath seen it. The coroner is one chosen by the Prince of the meaner sort of gentlemen...'

CASE STUDIES
Debt
Famous/infamous

Samuel Wesley, father of John, was arrested for debt and found himself in the debtors' prison within the walls of Lincoln Castle. Samuel's ruin started when he changed allegiances at a local election, first promising to support the representatives of the Dissenters, but then changing to support the church party when he learned of the aggressive attitudes of the Dissenters towards the church. When the electioneering and news of the rector's perceived turncoat decisions reached the Isle of Axholme, Samuel Wesley was in for a very hard time. When Samuel was visiting Lincoln he first had a scent of trouble to come, as he talked to a friend in the Castle Yard and was told that his own parishioners were hunting for him, and that one had said they would 'squeeze his guts out' if they found him. After this, a campaign of terror was launched against Wesley and his growing family in Epworth.

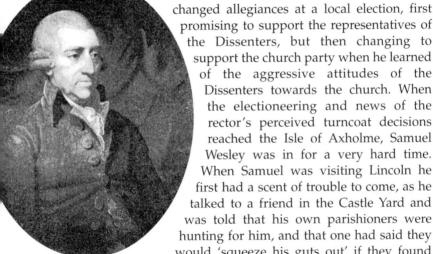

John Howard, the prison reformer. Author's collection

It started with a mob outside the rectory and pistols being fired; his children were frightened. He was then arrested for debt, initially for a sum of around £30; his flax at home was burned, the door of the rectory damaged, and his cows stabbed. There he was, locked up in Lincoln Castle, writing letters home, knowing that his own family were being half-starved and terrorised. In a letter, he gives an account of the arrest:

> On Friday last, when I had been christening a child at Epworth, I was arrested in my churchyard by one who had been my servant, and gathered my tithe last year, at the suit of one of Mr Whichcott's friends… the sum was not £30; but it was as good as five hundred. Now, they knew the burning of my flax, my London journey, and their throwing me out of my regiment had both sunk my credit and exhausted my money.

Yet even in the prison, Samuel kept busy and pressed on with good work. He writes about reading prayers twice a day and preaching on Sunday. He was sociable as ever, 'getting to know' his 'gaolbirds' as he said, and writing to the Society for Promoting Christian Knowledge for some books to give away. The working of the law was simple and inflexible: a debtor stayed in prison until the debt was paid. But most men in Samuel's situation would have no hope of clearing the debt; at least he had some powerful allies. Making himself busy helping the less fortunate was indeed a charitable thing to do, as many of the poorer debtors would be there for very long periods, and some would be in irons. Things had not changed much by 1776, when the prison reformer, John Howard, noted that 60% of prisoners in England's gaols were debtors.

The most horrendous experience of the whole sorry time must surely by the desperately tragic events of Wednesday 30 May 1705, when a mob came to the rectory firing guns and drumming in the 'rough music' tradition of English culture, and they were under the window where Susannah had given birth just a few weeks before. Samuel had taken the child to a neighbouring woman who acted as nurse. But this nurse lay over the baby and suffocated it in her sleep. When she woke up and found the corpse, she panicked and ran, screaming with fear, to Wesley and gave the baby to his servants. Then, the end of this agonising event comes with the dead baby being given to its mother. As Samuel reported it, the child was given to her 'before she was well awake, 'thrown 'cold and dead' into her arms.

His debts totalled £300, a very large sum then. He wrote about his problems to Archbishop Sharpe of York, and that good man helped him, both with money and with petitioning for help. Samuel was in the prison for approximately six months, after a Mr Hoar paid him £95 and the Archbishop added more. Back in Epworth he learned how his wife had survived; she had sent him her wedding ring while he was imprisoned, and he had sent it back, but somehow she fed the family and kept morale high enough to carry on. She had had no money at all, and the food was mostly the bread and milk yielded from her glebe. But the poor man with a sickly wife and eight children had pulled through.

Significance of the County Courts

In August 1845, the new system of dealing with minor debt at the county courts was shown to be most effectual in the case of Wood v. Rock. Rock wanted the sum of £55 as a recovery of a debt from Wood, who had been a tenant of Guy's Hospital, living on some land called Buck's Castle in Hereford (so the case was heard at the Oxford circuit). When Rock wanted to sell the land, he was told he had to have permission of the hospital steward. Rock wanted to buy the land and a lawyer was brought in, but he went ahead. Money was raised from an independent party – £55 – to put down as part-payment. But Wood remained in possession of the property and he was given a bill. He complained that he could not pay anything to anyone as the land could not be sold without the required permission.

In court, the result was: 'The counsel for the plaintiff proceeded to answer the learned gentleman's objections when HIS LORDSHIP intimated that there was sufficient evidence that the contract was rescinded by mutual consent.'

A few years before this, the case could easily have resulted in Wood being placed in a debtors' prison until he could raise funds.

Deserters

Desertion per se
Robert Bonner was one of a family of navvies working in Lincolnshire on the Fossdyke, the low land below Lincoln on the plain stretching towards Nottinghamshire. When General Whittam's regiment mustered on Canwick Common in 1741 Robert enlisted. But for reasons unknown, he deserted. When caught he was at first put in a cell at the castle, but his fate was to be shot by firing squad. He was taken to a tent at Canwick for the night before the execution, and then in the morning he walked out to face a squad of twelve musketeers.

He knelt on one knee, and then bravely dropped a handkerchief when he was ready to die.

For narratives of this kind in the years before c. 1800, one of the easiest sources is the *Gentleman's Magazine,* which had a section in every issue on 'Domestic occurrences' in which such topics as duels, trials, suspicious deaths and army matters, are listed. Later, in the nineteenth century, the *Annual Register* also had similar accounts of crimes.

Desertion and more serious crime

George Battrick was indicted in 1833 for having deserted his crew at Buenos Aires. The case was heard by the Solicitor General under an act of parliament that made it illegal for a captain to leave his crew at a foreign port. Witnesses were called and it was found that the *Hebe* had left from Liverpool to Argentina and had dropped her cargo there. The crew then found a drunk on the beach, and he was a sailor from another vessel, the *Lavinia.* They took him on board their longboat, intending to deliver him to his own ship.

There was then a storm. They could not reach the *Lavinia* and had to take refuge on an island; they had to use a piece of pig-iron as an anchor and this did not work. They woke up next day to find that the ship had broken free and floated some distance away. They then saw the defendant, Battrick, on board the *Hebe* and there was a row. He claimed that he had engaged some more hands and did not need them. When asked if he was going to leave the men floating adrift and without a captain, Battrick said, 'Yes I'll be damned if I don't.'

Apparently it was common for captains to leave their men in such predicaments and the courts were coming down hard on that. *The Times* report stated: 'Deserters of this description were very frequent among the vessels at Buenos Aires. The captain considered that the men had deserted and had therefore engaged others to supply their places…' The Lord Chief Justice found the captain guilty and he served a term in gaol.

Drunks

'Drunk and disorderly' – twenty shilling fine

In 1870, Francis Blood, who was a member of the Junior United Services Club, was arrested by PC Brook at one in the morning as the man had drawn a sword from a sword-stick and was threatening the

Marlborough Street police court (now a hotel). The author

other bystanders. One of the intended victims insisted on pressing charges, and Francis was taken into custody. Under arrest, Francis said he had no intention to hurt anyone but it was only a joke. The two men he had stopped were foreigners, and one, a Mr Kuhner, said he saw Francis flourishing the sword 'and wanted him taken into custody to find out if that sort of thing was allowed in this country'.

But Francis had clearly been on a binge-drinking session and he was trouble; he damaged items in the police cell and so he was given a fine of twenty shillings, with another five shillings for damage to the cell.

Drunk and violent – two months' hard labour

In April 1870, Richard Morris was in Marlborough Street police court. He had assaulted Joseph Soper outside a beer shop and, when approached by a constable, Morris assaulted him. He kicked the constable and ran off, but was arrested the nest day. He was sentenced to two months' hard labour.

Chapter 1

VARIETIES OF HOMICIDE

MURDER AND ATTEMPTED MURDER

In 1849 there was a blue book publication of the criminal tables. *The Times* noted that '640 capital offences have been pronounced during the last ten years – from 1839 to 1848. The offences were murder, malicious wounding, arson, riot, sodomy, burglary, returning from transportation and high treason. Of the sixty persons sentenced to death in 1848, only twelve were executed – ten males and two females. The offence was, in very case, murder of the most atrocious kind, the motive being principally revenge and jealousy.' That is a very significant statement regarding the history of serious crime. Thirty years previously there had been over 200 capital crimes on the statute books and by 1861 there would be only four, thanks to the Criminal Law Consolidation Act: murder, high treason, arson in a royal dockyard and piracy. Murder was always the number one capital crime.

The word 'murder' resonates with terror, drama and true crime best-sellers, but in more sober legal language it is the unlawful killing of a human being with malice aforethought, the death occurring within a year and a day. This focuses on a state of mind which is necessary to murder. The mind of a murderer, in law called the mens rea, may take various forms, but an intent to do grievous bodily harm may be enough to equate with the mens rea of killing. Until 1957, the notion of 'constructive malice' – causing a death in the execution of another crime – was still murder.

In terms of finding criminal ancestors who committed murder, there will be little difficulty in store. Murder cases are widely reported in the press and in a mass of printed secondary sources. As time has gone on, the amount of source material has in some ways proliferated and expanded. Before c.1750 most of the literature of murder was in broadsides, handbills and ballads as well as in official trial records. But since the advent of the periodical press and regional publishing, there has been a rapid expansion of material relating to the literature of homicide. In the twentieth century, after the advent of the courts of criminal appeal in 1907, there has been even more printed matter – and the possibility of having lots of varying sources of information with bias and distortion.

Until 1964 murder was a capital offence and the last two hangings were on 13 August that year: Peter Allen at Strangeways prison and Gwynne Evans at Liverpool; the last death sentence was passed on 1 November 1965, on David Chapman, in Leeds, but that was commuted to life imprisonment. On 8 November 1965 the Murder (Abolition of Death Penalty) Act was passed. But in the search for skeletons in the cupboard in the years between c.1600 and c.1860 if the ancestor was a murderer then the researcher may well have to read the chronicles of hanging. In recent years there has been a mass of

An early chapbook on murder for a popular audience. Author's collection

publications, including some from the memoirs of the hangmen and prison officers who were present.

The detective work in family history when it comes to murder may well be in the tracing of the felons who were reprieved. That would lead in most cases to transportation (up to 1867), to life imprisonment or to asylum records. Prison records in that case are clearly the most substantial resource. The most profitable sequence of research gambits is as follows:

• When the crime is established, read the newspaper reports.
• Back this up with court records.
• If there was an appeal, find the appeal court records
• For other destinations of the felon, go to prison or transportation records.
• For more modern cases, there will be memoirs from lawyers, judges, police officers and memoirists.

Attempted murder was dropped as a capital offence in the Offences Against the Person Act of 1861. The repealed capital offences included attempts in terms of poisoning, damaging a building, arson, casting away a ship and attempting to shoot or drown. The Criminal Attempts Act of 1981 defined attempt as 'an intent to commit an offence... a person commits an act which is more than merely preparatory to the commission of the offence.'

FELO DE SE: SUICIDE

An old term for suicide is 'self-murther' and that encapsulates the legal idea. One's own body is not one's spiritual property, as it were. Penal process used to follow a suicide, in that the body could not be buried in consecrated ground. There was also the advent of a suicide pact, which involved one person influencing another to take their life, and when suicide itself ceased to be a criminal offence in 1961, a suicide pact remained a crime. Not long before this reform, in 1957, 514,870 people died and of these, 5,315 were suicides.

As Sir Harold Scott, writing just before the 1961 reforms:

> Until recently there was much preoccupation with its [suicide's] rightness or wrongness, but little on its essential causes. During the last hundred years or so, science has directed its attention to suicide as an aspect of human behaviour amenable to analysis.

'Famous Crimes' magazine. Author's collection.

Whilst a great deal of knowledge has emerged from the intensive study carried out... it is admitted on all hands that suicide is still something of an enigma.

Concise Encyclopaedia of Crime and Criminals, 1961

Throughout history, suicide has been an act of shame; the coroners' courts give clear support to this. In a case reported in the *Leeds Mercury* in 1865, a coroner's court had heard that James Smith had thrown himself into the River Aire with pockets weighted with stones - but still the jury was not convinced that this was suicide – so extreme was the following stigma attached to him and his family. The verdict recorded was 'found drowned'.

Sources are mainly in newspapers and periodicals, inquest papers, police records and in Home Office correspondence and State papers. Therefore there is no dearth of literature on the subject, and the changing attitudes over the centuries needs to be understood as part of the research, as this is clearly one example of the need to know the social and moral contexts. My uncle took his own life, as I stated in the introduction. I vividly recall the silence, the shame and the lack of any discourse on the subject. His embezzlement of funds preceded his suicide and so there was a double negativity and loss of social face built into the whole case, particularly in a close-knit village community. Such tales are quite common throughout British history, and they are more frequent as capital economy and mass market industrialism developed, opening up opportunities and temptations for fraudulent crime.

MANSLAUGHTER

This is a crime of unlawful homicide and has two varieties: voluntary is a killing with malice aforethought but with the presence of a mitigating factor at the time; and involuntary, where the killing was done without malice but with a fault element – that is, the death was caused in the course of another act. In historical periods there have been various versions of this, including acts encompassing self-defence and participation in an affray. In the nineteenth century in particular, the defences of provocation and temporary insanity were attempted in court but often with little success. In adversarial trials, clearly there would be attempts to show that a mens rea was absent in a suspicious death.

INFANTICIDE

Infanticide, the killing of a newborn child, was made a version of manslaughter, rather than murder, in 1938, with a factor of mental anguish and depression being involved. It ceased to be a capital offence in 1922. Previously, there had been a very large number of cases, and also the offence of concealing a child; both were in most cases related to post-natal depression at times when such a concept did not exist. But in the mid-Victorian period there was an effort to send the young mothers involved into care of some kind, rather than to the scaffold, as happened in many cases up to the 1830s.

PETTY TREASON

This 'little treason' was a concept related to the notion of authority and the social hierarchy, so that, if a wife murdered a husband or a servant murdered a master, the punishment if convicted would be burning at the stake rather than hanging. The male master of a household was conceived as the representative of royal authority and so his murder would be defined as a version of treason. It was abolished in 1790 and became part of the crime of murder. But even after that, in the famous Courvoisier case of 1840, when Lord William Russell was found murdered in his bed, and by his butler, the case

The Drop at Newgate. Author's collection

was a major sensation and 40,000 people turned up to watch Courvoisier hang. Before 1790, women who killed their husbands would be drawn on a hurdle to a place of execution and burned. It was common practice for the hangman to strangle the culprit (for a small fee) before the tying at the stake was done.

CANNIBALISM

As the title of a 1960s novel reminded us, *Eating People is Wrong*. But what was to be done in times past when extreme privation and the threat of death by starvation made cannibalism essential? A taboo has been broken, and nothing more, if the corpse was not murdered, of course. Otherwise, a murder followed by the eating of flesh is something else entirely. The most celebrated case study of the nineteenth century is arguably that of Captain John Dudley in 1884. He was on a longboat, starving to death, 1,600 miles off land in Africa, and he killed the cabin boy, Richard Parker, to eat him. Dudley survived but faced a charge of murder. He was sentenced to death but of course he had a sort of defence, claiming that the killing was a 'necessity'. He was reprieved and the sentence commuted to six months.

DIMINISHED RESPONSIBILITY AND INSANITY DEFENCES

In 1843, Daniel McNaghten shot dead the private secretary to Sir Robert Peel, Edward Drummond. He was acquitted on the grounds of insanity and so the concept of 'McNaghten's Rules' entered criminal law. These were to be a measure of ascertaining if a defendant was sane or insane in the course of a killing. Of course, if used as a defence and successful, the likely result was a stay in an asylum 'for Her Majesty's pleasure.' Even in more recent times, this has been a difficult concept to handle in court. In the years 1977-86, around 300 people in Britain were detained as 'unfit to plead'. Writing in 1996, Oliver Cyriax, made the point that a quarter of those were still in hospital awaiting trial.

Naturally, these cases link to acts of suicide, and therefore coroners' courts are a source of information as well as the main criminal courts. But in contrast to inanity, the defence of diminished responsibility gradually emerged. This was defined as 'A defence to a charge of murder that a person was suffering from such abnormality of mind as substantially impaired his mental responsibility for his acts and omissions in killing, or being a party to a killing of another...' Before that concept even existed, there are cases in which other words have been used to exonerate the accused, as in a case in Bradford.

It reads like such a simple, uncomplicated statement of a killing: 'York Assizes: Abraham Bairstan, aged 60, was put to the bar, charged with the wilful murder of Sarah Bairstan his wife, in the parish of Bradford.' In the busy, overworked courts of the regency, dealing with new and often puzzling crimes form the labouring classes in the fast-growing towns, it was maybe just another 'domestic' that went too far. But this is far from the truth, and the Bairstan case gives us an insight into the plight of those unfortunate people at the time who were victims of ignorance as well as of illness. In this instance it was an awful, anguished mental illness that played a major part in this murder.

When the turnkey brought Bairstan into the court he commented that he had not heard the prisoner say a word since he was brought to York and locked up. This was nothing new to the man's family. Mr Baron Hullock, presiding, was shocked but also full of that natural curiosity of someone who just does not understand something. He pressed the gaoler to explain. He asked if the man in the dock understood the spoken word, and the answer was no. He also ascertained that Bairstan appeared to have no response to any sound whatsoever, nor any movement.

It makes painful reading in the court report to note that the prisoner was a 'dull and heavy looking man who... cast a vacant glance around the court'. The reporter in 1824 noted that the man 'appeared totally insensible of the nature of the proceedings'.

Poor Hullock had a real challenge to try to communicate with the man, trying his best to make the prisoner make any sound at all, asking several questions but receiving no answer. When he asked 'Do you hear what I say to you?' Bairstan simply stared at the officer next to him.

It was obviously going to be one of those trials at which many people were thinking that this silence was the best ruse if a man wanted to avoid the rope. The judge had to instruct the jury about potential fraud and the possibility that this was a tough and amoral killer with a canny wit and impressive acting skills. In legal jargon, the point was, was the man standing there fraudulently, wilfully and obstinately, or 'by the act and providence of God?' It was going to be a hard task, one might think, but not so: enter his sons and a close friend. They told a very sad story, and an astounding one, given that Bairstan managed to marry and raise a family.

His friend stated that he had known the prisoner for over fifty years, and that he was sure that ten years had passed since Bairstan had fallen silent. He explained that his two sons had been looking after the old man in that time. His key statement was that 'while he was sane, his wife and he had lived together very comfortably'. The man, Jeremiah Hailey, added that his friend had been capable of merely saying yes or no, and that the last time he had heard the man speak was when he had asked him if he knew his friend Jeremiah. 'He said aye, but I think he did not know me.'

Bairstan's two sons confirmed that their father had been silent in that ten-year period, only excepting one or two words. Henry said that since being locked up, his father had been pressed to speak and had answered something sounding like 'Be quiet... be quiet'. The other son, Joseph, confirmed that his father had been 'out of his mind' for ten years.'

There had been enough in him to marry and earn a living, but we must see with hindsight and more relevant knowledge, that Abraham Bairstan had been struck by a paralysis, perhaps combined with a depressive mental illness. In 1824, the most meaningful explanation was to put it down to God's will, so the jury found that the prisoner stood mute 'by the visitation of God'.

Or, if one is pressed to say that it had all been a wonderfully impressive family performance, then would not this be the sure way to keep the old man from the noose? On the other hand, he was destined to be shut away for ever in awful conditions, being criminally insane. The truth will perhaps never now be known.

RESEARCH PROCESS

For all the above homicide cases, the process and the sources fall in line and encompass mostly the same patterns of research. Murder cases and all equally serious crimes against the person are in the assize records, and the essential process for this is to be sure in what circuit the case was tried. During the centuries up to 1971 when there were assizes at the heart of the criminal justice system, the circuits were six, and covered all areas except the Palatinates (Cheshire, Durham and Lancashire, with the addition of

Middlesex) but in 1864 these were reshuffled so that from that date we have:

- Home and Norfolk – making the South Eastern
- A North Eastern Circuit was formed and Lancashire came into that circuit
- Wales was split into North and South Divisions

Previously, as will be seen in *The Times* law reports up to 1864, the circuits were named in the reports, and these courts were held twice a year at Spring and Autumn, being comprised of: Norfolk, Midland, Northern, Home, Oxford and Western. Within those circuits, the murder case searched for would be heard at the nearest to the offence in most cases, so that the Oxford circuit included Oxford, Reading, Worcester, Stafford, Shrewsbury, Hereford, Monmouth and Gloucester.

It may be seen from this that once the murder in question is known and located, the process in following the whole process of law, from trial to sentence, is this:

Phase one: find the location of the trial. A crime committed in Lincolnshire was usually heard at Lincoln, but be aware that sometimes a crime committed in Nottingham was also heard at Lincoln.

Phase Two: study the assize records, at county record offices or at The National Archives, as summarized in the introduction.

Phase three: also check press reports and accounts in *The Annual Register* (Up to the mid Victorian period this had full accounts of most trials and cases). The press reports are most easily accessed by consulting The Times Digital Archive.

Phase Four: find appeal court records if the case goes to appeal. Before 1907 many cases can be found in Crown Cases Reserved – in print as *Cox's Crown Cases Reserved*. These will refer to the case history of the affair.

Phase Five: finally, follow the trial outcome – go either to prison records, transportation records or execution accounts.

A special note on reprieves and pardons
Note that the Home Office has been in existence since 1782, and that for the bulk of the period in which assize courts and others are easily accessible (and in English) judges would recommend mercy and

The Recorder's Office, where the fate of condemned felons on appeal rested. Author's collection

decisions would be made either by the Home Secretary and the Sovereign, together with the Recorder of London. For research purposes, letters asking for pardon are available at The National Archives in the HO series, petitions for pardon and reprieves.

All the crimes in this chapter will have been heard at assizes, or at the Old Bailey, the Central Criminal Court. The Old Bailey records are accessible online and are searchable, free, so there are plenty of trial transcripts here, in addition to accounts by gaol ordinaries (keepers or turnkeys) about the criminals involved.

It is important to note, however, that some serious crime cases were heard not at assizes but in various superior courts: these are the higher courts in the system, up to the House of Lords. Therefore, a case happening at sea might have been heard in an Admiralty Court, for instance. The best way to find out where the case was heard is to start with the press report. These will state the court location of the trial and also give the names of the judge or judges.

CASE STUDIES
Murder (pre- 1861)
Edward Hall liked a drink. In fact he liked to have an enormous quantity of drink, and that always led him into trouble. In July 1831, it led him to the gallows in Lincoln.

Hall, just twenty-two, was out filling himself with beer one June evening in Grimsby and he made too much noise for Edward Button, living near the alehouses where hall had a good time. Hall was making a nuisance of himself in a pub run by a Mr Kempsley and Button came to help the landlord throw the drunkard out into the street. After Hall was turfed out, Button still kept on his case, shouting through a window, 'Take him to the gaol, the rascal deserves to go for making such a row on a Sunday night.' Button was being a good citizen, expressing his moral views openly. The problem was that Hall felt that deeply and he vowed revenge.

'I'll kill Kempsley and somebody else!' he roared as he sharpened a knife on a stone a few days later. A witness heard him make that awful oath. A man called Milner, who spent time with hall, monitored the progress of the man's rankling hatred of the landlord and of Button.

Nothing much happened for a few days but on 2 July, Milner went out drinking with a man called Joseph Nash and also with Edward Button. They went along to the Duke of York, run by a Mrs Dines, and much later on, near midnight, Hall and his friend Ratton came in; Hall was in a raucous mood, out to provoke Button and he succeeded. The talk went like this, according to a witness: Button said, 'Hello! What do you want?'

'One bully has as much right here as another,' Hall answered, and Button followed that with a blow to Hall's face. Milner said that at first Button never even moved from his chair, but soon after there was a direct confrontation. Hall strode across to the far corner of the inn and challenged his enemy. 'I'm ready for you any time!'

A Lincoln pamphlet on the event reports the fight as being a desperate affair: 'In a short time both parties fell to the floor; they fell in the doorway leading from one room into another, there was no light in the other room, but it was not very dark where they fell…'

What happened next must be a familiar tale from many a drunken brawl: one of the men had a knife, and of course, it was Hall. From the struggle on the floor, Button emerged, staggering into the light for all to see; then he managed to walk to a chair and there he sat down, clearly in great pain and bleeding. Someone at the scene said that he ground his teeth together and then died instantly.

A man opened Button's waistcoat because the crowd thought he was having a fit, but then the blood was evident and the man 'saw a wound on the fellow's breast'. The landlady screamed out loud that a man had been stabbed. As for Hall, in his drink he still had the wit to try to throw away the weapon; he appears to have gone outside to do that and they go back inside the inn where someone accused him: 'Hall, you have stabbed this man with a knife.' Hall said he had no knife on him.

Cobb Hall, Lincoln Castle, a hanging-place. The author

Naturally, everyone there knew that he had been outside to throw away the murder weapon. Later in court, the daughter of the landlady said that she heard Hall provoke Button, saying, 'Come on!' She said he had one arm behind him – that was where he held the knife. She said that she followed the fight, holding a candle, and she said that she saw Hall holding Button fast to the ground, with a knee on him, and then the killer knocked away her candle. Before the light was out, though, she said, 'I saw a knife in Hall's hand.' She was not the only one there who saw that.

Evidence from the local surgeon confirmed that Button had suffered a deep two-inch long wound by his sternum and the knife 'had passed through the integuments in an oblique direction, upwards and inwards, entering between the fifth and sixth ribs'. The doctor stated that there was no doubt that the knife wound had caused the death of the deceased. In court, all this was heard in silence by the man in the dock, and he had nothing to say before a guilty verdict was passed on him.

The reporter in court noted that, 'The prisoner, during the whole of the trial, preserved a remarkable indifference to his fate, but afterwards he manifested a very different spirit.' That was after the judge donned the black cap and sentenced Hall to hang. The judge commented on 'the premeditated malice in the prisoner's mind, in having, on two separate occasions, sharpened a knife with a cool and deliberate intent to use such a weapon against one, if not two persons...'

The reporter went on, saying that Hall's behaviour was then 'truly becoming, neither displaying excess of timidity not unbecoming confidence, but looked forward to his approaching fate with calmness and resignation'. The assembled crowd by the tower at Cobb Hall, Lincoln Castle, had what they thought was good entertainment, many paying for the best views of the hanging from the inns across the road. They even enjoyed a long sermon on the sins of the condemned man. This was on 22 July 1831, and Hall must have wished he could have had more than the traditional final drink of ale at The Struggler public house by the castle walls.

Murder (Twentieth Century)
Notice that this case includes both assizes and appeal court.

On a summer's day in 1908, the city of Bradford was shocked by the breaking news of a brutal murder, and it was most disturbing as it happened in the afternoon. Thomas Wilkinson, working at Fieldhouse and Jowett in Swain Street, was beaten to death by someone wielding a poker, and the killer had brought the weapon with him, as there was no coal fire in the store.

The murderer was not exactly careful to cover his tracks or to hide his identity in any way; not only had he been seen standing in the doorway by a passer-by, looking troubled, and actually saying that 'They were having a bit of bother in the office,' but he also bought the poker just down the road, as Samuel Ellis, who sold him the weapon, was to testify.

From these details, it would appear that there may not have been a motive, as it was the nasty work of someone who was distracted in the extreme, but there was in fact a clear motive. The killer was John Ellwood, and he had worked for Fieldhouse and Jowett, leaving that employment about six months before this incident. He had been involved in a heated row with his employers and had left under a cloud; it was therefore not hard for the police to show that, as an employee, he would know the routine of the place in a typical week, and would therefore be aware that large amounts of money were brought to the building by the company cashier every Friday. It was no coincidence, perhaps, that Ellwood had arranged to visit the premises at two o'clock that afternoon, Friday 31 July. There had been correspondence, and both Ellwood and Wilkinson had written or rung up to leave messages. There was also the testimony of the landlord of the Fountain Brewery, who had seen the accused leave his pub just before the time of the killing.

It was hardly going to be a problem for the investigating officers, as there was plenty of blood on Ellwood's clothes when he was arrested, and his pathetic excuse that the cause of this was merely a bleeding nose was not going to fool anyone. His line of thought regarding his reasons for being seen at the murder scene that day by the man going by (he was Isaac Pollard) was simply that Wilkinson was trying to have him reinstated in his post; Mrs Ellwood produced evidence of a letter from Wilkinson to that effect, and also stated that her husband had been with her at home at the time of the murder.

All fairly straightforward, we might think. When he appeared at Leeds Assizes on 12 November that year, and it was discussed that Ellwood's intention was to have a wages cheque, intended for the employees of the mills, to be cashed. Ellwood, it was claimed, was planning to rob Wilkinson of that cash. Later, at appeal, it was stated that a witness who had been bound over to attend the trial had not actually been called, and the lawyers at the time argued that this evidence would not have been helpful for the defence case.

At the Court of Appeal on 20 November, Mr Gregory Ellis, for the applicant Ellwood, argued that at the trial there was no motive for the murder defined and explained. The supposed letter from Wilkinson inviting him to come regarding a job had been dismissed, but Ellwood's defence brought this up again. Mr Justice Channel explained the situation, as Ellwood stood and wondered if he was to be saved from the noose, that,' … there is a great deal of difference between absence of proved motive and proved absence of motive'. In other words, that the accused planned to go to the premises and steal, and to steal even at the cost of a life, appeared to be the motive, and no letter arranging a meeting would cast doubt on that. After all, he had been seen by a man at the time, and it was known that he had bought the poker. There was no ambiguity in the material evidence of the nature of the killing: the victim was battered brutally and relentlessly, the wounds inflicted by the poker.

The appeal was refused. John Ellwood became another client of executioner Henry Pierrepoint, and he was hanged on 3 December 1908 at Armley Gaol.

Attempted Murder

The important point in this story is that this was well before 1861, and attempted murder – particularly by a woman – was seen as totally reprehensible. The affair had to go to a reprieve at the highest level. The system at this time was that the recorder's office would hold a 'hanging council' with the Home Secretary and the fate of those recommended for mercy would be decided there.

Elizabeth Ward was only seventeen when she very nearly killed her sister-in-law. She was destined to hang for it and, in spite of a plea to the judge, he would not commute the sentence, despite her youth. He thought she should be an exemplar case to deter others. *The Times* reported the case, picking out this aspect: 'One enormous case occurred at York – that of Elizabeth Ward, seventeen years of age, who was convicted of the horrid crime of administering poison to her sister, and is to suffer death.' The newspaper got the facts slightly wrong, but it picked out the repugnance of the affair.

In July 1816 Elizabeth went from her home in Rothwell into Leeds (only a few miles away) and bought two ounces of arsenic. She was seen the next day mixing white powder into a milk and oatmeal porridge, and she was seen by her little brother George, whose statements later would be very important. Her sister-in-law Charlotte was the intended victim, and the fact that she noticed something amiss with the food is quite astonishing through modern eyes. Most poison victims were unlikely to do this, of course, as the natural inclination is to eat or drink with ease and with speed. But Charlotte for some reason sensed something wrong. She noticed the white substance in the jug, then locked it in a cupboard. Even more impressive was her forcing herself to be sick to vomit up what tiny traces had gone into her blood. As for Elizabeth, she was seen by little George throwing the rest of the food away.

Sensible Charlotte then went for medical advice and consulted a druggist, Mark Poskitt. He and another chemist tested vomit and found arsenic traces. The teenager had failed in her quest to kill, but it had been a close-run thing. In most cases, the victim would have swallowed enough to kill or at least to create long hours of horrible suffering. Elizabeth was charged, naturally. There was a motive, and the girl explained this herself when questioned, saying that after Elizabeth's mother had died a few months before these events, Charlotte had become the centre of power in the home and young Elizabeth did not like that at all. But Charlotte came through the effects of the small amount of poison she had taken and went to the magistrate to give the facts.

Nine-year-old George had to testify against his big sister, and he had plenty to say. This was at York Assizes, just a week after the attempted murder. It is stunning to report that there was no defence lawyer for the girl, and yet five witnesses were called. The teenager was allowed to question these people but as we can imagine, she could not put much of a coherent argument together and could simply protest her innocence. There were three druggists lined up against her, and the one from whom she had bought the arsenic in Leeds recognised her: she was doomed.

One odd aspect of the case, as pointed out by historian Katherine Watson, is that Poskitt had no experience of the kind of pathology required in poisoning cases and said that he had learned all he knew from books only. Watson notes also, 'It is also interesting to note that Sutcliffe (a druggist) lived in York, the seat of the assize court: the fact that Poskitt gave him the sample to test indicates that the apothecary was determined to obtain corroboration of his findings.'

All the girl could say after all this science lined up against her was, 'I am innocent of the crime.' There were several charges against her. Attempted murder was a capital offence under Lord Ellenborough's Act of 1803; she had given poison in a deadly quantity and although there was no evidence of her intention, there was no defence to say otherwise. But she was sentenced to death, and only then did another story come through. There may well have been a case of insanity in this, but the judge found no reason to commute the sentence: he could have done, and most murder cases ended in a commutation at that time. It was to be a case of a reprieve.

Even that process was long and uncertain. The sovereign, George III, was mentally incapacitated and the appeal went to the Home Secretary, Lord Sidmouth and then to the Regent. There was support for the girl in high places, though, and here there was a Yorkshire lobby, from no less a dignitary than Lord Lascelles. He it was who brought about a postponement of the hanging at first, and then with more time, the city of York and other groups across the county put together a petition that went to the Prince Regent, who directed a reprieve. (A feature of this is the highly unusual reprieve process.)

Suicide
Infamous – the end of the White Mischief case
It is not widely known that the end of the story of one of the most intriguing and celebrated murder cases of the twentieth century happened in Liverpool at the grand and stylish Adelphi Hotel in 1942. It was there that Sir Jock Delves Broughton took his own life. The story was that of the murder of Lord Errol in Kenya in 1941, whose body was found in a car in January of that year, with a bullet lodged in his brain.

The irony of the place of his death is not hard to miss. The Adelphi is huge and palatial; a visit there now evokes the glamour and excitement of the great age of the ocean liners; in the 1940s it would have had some of that glamour. In the midst of the ballroom dances and the ebb and flow of immigrants and fugitives from war, the inscrutable old drinker and bon viveur exited the world. There is something fitting there in the effete and somehow pathetic figure dying in that place.

The Adelphi Hotel, Liverpool, where the suicide took place. The author

In the film *White Mischief*, the murder and the tale of the affair that caused it is told with high drama and passion; there were certainly elements of that in the real tragedy of this threesome of older man, attractive young wife and dashing lover. But there was also a large element of what we now see as sordid and sad. The affair is all the more fascinating because Broughton was the only real suspect and yet the murder is unsolved to this day. Broughton insisted on his innocence, writing to an aunt in 1941 as follows:

> I was just a victim of unfortunate circumstances… some clever person took advantage of an unrivalled opportunity of getting rid of Erroll and… throwing all suspicion on me.

'Jock' as he was known, had married Diana Caldwell in Durban in November 1940 at a registry office. From there they went to Kenya. He had promised to let her have £5,000 a year. Then she went on to enjoy herself with Lord Erroll, and Jock's torment began. There was something inevitable about the course of Erroll's life, from the affair through to his being shot on the Ngong to Nairobi road. What made Broughton so intriguing a character was the fact that he had been hired by MI6, and that he had a Somali driver who worked for him, leading to the theory that this driver could easily have been in the back of the car that night, and could have done the required execution.

Broughton's descent after the acquittal from the murder charge led him to Liverpool. He had always been a heavy drinker, but now he was intensely so, and he boarded ship for Liverpool in October 1942 in a rotten state; he was still full of venom, and cabled his friend Colville from the ship saying of his former wife, Diana, 'You've got the bitch, now buy her the kennel.' He was angry and vengeful, writing that he would let it be known that Diana had perpetrated an insurance false claim some years before. The desperate and raging lord must have felt that this was his final journey: he had only been in Liverpool for just over a month when he took his own life. A morphine overdose was to end the life of this notorious aristocrat.

Even in death, however, there was mystery around the man. The Liverpool coroner had been given possession of a letter written by Broughton to be given to him after the man's death, and the coroner never made the contents of this public. But with regard to the anticlimax of the manner of Broughton's death in Liverpool, it must be said that according to one line of thought, the whole thing was in fact a murder and had been fabricated as a suicide. The theory goes that Broughton knew too much from his past in espionage and the matter should be seen in terms of the politics of the time and his life in Africa. The outcome, if we believe this speculation, is that he had to be removed from the scene, and that the OSS (Office of Strategic Services) had made sure that a particular drug was taken that fateful night. As Errol Trzebinski has said, the Liverpool coroner would have been expected to know where the fatal drugs came from. Perhaps he had no idea. What we are left with is a spy story, one involving a man who was maybe involved in a 'hit' job of Errol, but who was just a pawn. Here was a man who was suspected of being a fraud, and surely weighed down by guilt.

His character has been summed up by historian David Cannadine in this way: '… another dim and vain Etonian, with fifteen thousand acres in Cheshire and Staffordshire… He evaded military service in 1914 on the grounds of sunstroke, and brought the Spring Valley estate in Kenya in 1923. His purpose in life was to have a good time.'

There was no good time that night in the Adelphi when he reached the end of the line. If it was suicide, it was a crime of course, then. Until 1961 suicide was still an offence in the eyes of the law. The palatial Adelphi, was pride of the city in several incantations since James Rradley built the first hotel there in 1826. The new Adelphi which was there when Jock arrived was the delight of the great hotelier Arthur Towle who would be have been shuddering with shame at the stigma of a suicide within those grand marble walls. Sad, everyday Victorian

An Everyday Case

In Leeds in 1868, at the corner's court, the case was heard of Matthew Atkin, fifty-nine years old, who was found in his own home with his throat cut. He was a tailor and he had been seriously ill, most recently having gone virtually blind. He had become deeply depressed by the loss of sight and, in the early hours of one morning, he was not in bed; his wife found him lying in the cellar with a deep gash in his throat. He had cut his own jugular artery. The verdict was suicide whilst temporarily insane.

Manslaughter

The following two law reports provide a sharp contrast regarding the difficulties of defining and describing the offence in the early nineteenth century.

First, at the Hertford assizes in 1816, the Crown side heard the tale of a boxing match. A labourer called Joseph Merriden was convicted of killing Joseph Rhoades in the ring; the story was that Rhoades had not wanted to fight but Merriden pushed the matter. They fought at Rickmansworth park for an hour and a half and then Rhoades fell, senseless; he died soon after. The sentence was just seven days in prison.

In contrast, at the Durham assizes in August 1818, the court heard the case of William Smith, who had broken a man's arm with a 'deadly weapon' and then struck Matthew Reed with it. The first charge was wilful murder, which appears to be accurate, but then, the jury found him guilty of manslaughter. The judge said to the man: 'It is my duty to tell you that if you are again guilty in the same way, that the law will not excuse it so.' The sentence was one year in prison.

Infanticide

At York in 1800, Mary Thorp, just twenty-two years old, pleaded not guilty to a charge of 'murdering her male infant'. It was the first capital offence tried in Yorkshire in the new century. One of the very first accounts of the case, published in 1831, is extant but keeps back much of the material around the story, simply pointing out that Mary began domestic service at fourteen, was happy, and then was seduced 'by one, whilst he pretended to lead the confiding girl on to happiness, brought her to ruin, misery and disgrace'. It appears from the records that there was no knowledge of the identity of this man.

That course of seduction and ruin is arguably the typology of the infanticide chronicle throughout centuries of English history. In Mary Thorp's case the events were chillingly simple: a woman friend helped in the birth of the child, and then, according to one reporter, a week later Mary took the child to a pond and threw it into the water, a stone tied around its neck. This appears to be too vague an account; she in fact stayed with a widow called Hartley in Sheffield, for the delivery, then said she was moving on to Derby to be with her sister. But her plan was to go to Ecclesfield. It was there, in the river near Bridge Houses, that the child was thrown to its death, with tape tied tightly around its neck.

The child had been strangled before it was thrown into the water, and there was no doubt that the tape around its neck was Mary's: Hartley identified the material. There was an inquest following this discovery of course; the charge was murder, and the coroner arranged for Mary Thorp to stand trial at York. The opinion of a commentator at the time was simple but powerful: 'The wretched girl became a miserable mother, and gave birth to a child whose smiles became her reproach.'

The defence was that the woman was not aware of what she was doing and was delirious. The medical men agreed that she had indeed suffered from 'milk fever' but that this was not sufficient cause of any palpable insanity in Mary. She had apparently intended to do the deed, and did so with awareness of the act. In spite of the fact that she did not look like a ragged victim of street poverty and likely immorality, the jury was not sympathetic, and took into consideration the circumstantial evidence, along with the point about no real insanity in Mary, and so reached a verdict of guilty.

When the sentence was passed, as reported by Thomas Rede

Leman, Mary 'bore it with great firmness and curtseyed very lowly to the court before she left it'. At the York Tyburn on 17 March she was hanged.

According to the first full report, the morality fixed as part of the judgement on Mary was entirely in keeping with the limited understanding of infanticide at the time: 'In a case like this, there can be no medium between pity for the offender, or utter abhorrence' yet the writer goes on to tackle the subject of her possible temporary insanity:

> Medical experience tells us that fevers of all descriptions affect the sanity of the sufferer: milk fever is most powerful in its effects; and though the law might condemn, society may pity such a criminal.

It is a sad story indeed. Mary in court was a 'pale and care-worn creature' and of course, she had been the subject of a heartless seduction. This pattern of behaviour, leading to child-murder, was to preoccupy the best minds of the later Victorian period; Elizabeth Gaskell wrote her novel, *Ruth*, in 1853, to deal with the difficult subject of the seduction of a poor working girl by a rich man. She lost friends over the publication.

In cases like that of Mary Thorp, then, the commentaries show a great deal of sympathy, and writers were clearly aware of the clash between criminal law and moral opinion. But all this was of no use to the condemned young woman, destined to die on the scaffold. We have to admire her resolve and self-control: when the verdict was given, she stood firm, and it was noted that 'In person she was extremely prepossessing.' It has to be said, with a more modern understanding of the dynamics of a courtroom, that she should have been less prepossessing and more frail and demure. It might have had some influence on those in judgement.

Petty Treason

Over the centuries, York Castle has witnessed some terrible scenes of human suffering, but few can equal the story of Elizabeth Broadingham. The narrative vaguely echoes the actions of Lady Macbeth lacking the 'milk of human kindness' except that the setting and the motives are the lowest and most despicable imaginable.

How women killers were depicted: Amelia Dyer. Author's collection

John Broadingham, her husband, was not exactly a pillar of the community. He was locked away in York dungeons for robbery when Elizabeth began her affair with Thomas Aikney, a man younger than she. It was a case of extreme passion, 'while the cat's away', and she liked the pleasures of loving and sex with the other man so much that she moved in with him.

A man coming out of prison after all kinds of deprivations expects some comfort and loyalty from his family. John Broadingham found none of this: he merely found that his wife had left the home. Elizabeth appears to have wanted more than simply living with Aikney as his partner; she wanted to be free of the marriage with John, and to remove the husband from the scene altogether was her aim.

She began to work on Aikney with a view to leading him into the murder of John. The younger man at first resisted these pleas and wiles, but after some time he began to be influenced. It is recounted, though not definitely known, that Elizabeth made sure that Aikney had plenty of alcohol in him and tempted him in all the ways she could invent, as he allured him into a murderous pact. He finally went along with the plan.

Elizabeth must have been a very influential speaker and something of an actress; not only had she inveigled her way into Aikney's life, she now played the part of good wife, returning to John and apparently wanting to return to the marital harmony they once had. John took her back. But only a week or so after moving back home, she was talking to Thomas Aikney about their plan, and sorting out the details of where and when it would be done. The lover still vainly tried to resist, but she was relentless. Poor Thomas thought that the best move was to run away and avoid the confrontation, to make a new start elsewhere.

Things came to a head on the night of 8 February 1776, when Elizabeth woke her husband as there was a loud noise downstairs; John staggered down to investigate and made his way to the door where Aikney was pounding on the wood. As John Broadingham opened up, Aikney knifed him in the chest and then, as the frenzied attack continued, he stabbed the man in the thigh and the leg. With the knife stuck in his belly, John managed to walk out into the street where he was seen by neighbours. So badly was the husband hurt that he had almost been eviscerated in the assault; he was clutching his stomach and his guts were exposed. The report at the time states that he was 'supporting his bowels'.

John Broadingham died the day after the attack. It took only a short time for neighbours and the magistrate to find Aikney and then the whole story was revealed. Elizabeth and Thomas confessed and he was hanged at York on 20 March. In this tale lies the incredible difference between punishment for murder and petty treason; Aikney's body, as was the custom, was cut down and then transported to Leeds Infirmary for use in dissection work with medical education. But Elizabeth had committed petty treason. Her fate was to be burnt at the stake. The only humane act in these cases was that the executioner normally strangled the woman before the fire was set alight, and he did so for Elizabeth. She was burnt and some ghoulish witnesses collected her ashes as souvenirs.

Mercy never entered into the matter when a woman was considered for the death penalty in the late eighteenth century and in the early nineteenth century. The great journalist of the period, J W Robertson Scott, has a memory of a woman on a scaffold at this time:

' … it was an old woman, a mere old wrinkled, wretched bundle. She was said to have killed a bastard. She cried, "You cannot hang me!" But they did.'

Burning for petty treason, as explained in the introduction, was abolished in 1790: too late for Elizabeth Broadingham.

Cannibalism

Cases were not always limited to desperate acts on the high seas. In 1869, at the Ryde Petty Sessions, Nicholas Boud, a shipbroker, was convicted of the offence. He was drunk and aggressive in the Black Horse Inn in Ryde, throwing drink at the landlady and creating an affray. When the landlady's son tried to eject Bond, the drunk bit him on the cheek, and the report of the affair notes that, 'Bond bit him so severely on the cheek, drawing blood, and leaving the marks of his teeth… He also took his finger in his mouth and bit it nearly to the bone.' The Bench found him guilty of cannibalism and the magistrate said: 'You have been guilty of a disgraceful act… unbecoming a man, much less and Englishman. He was given £5 costs or two months in prison.

A much more typical and celebrated case was that of Tom Dudley and Edwin Stephens, who were tried at Exeter assizes for murder on the high seas. The men had killed and eaten young Richard Parker on board the *Mignonette*. The act was seen as essential to preserve life and Dudley had said a prayer before cutting the young man's throat, and the defence was partly that Parker was believed to be dying anyway. At first, both men were sentenced to hang, but then this was commuted to six months in prison.

Diminished responsibility and insanity defences

Insanity in the court, in terms of the McNaghten rules (after 1843) was a tough subject to deal with. Even long before that date, there had been cases which show the humane side of the criminal justice system, as of course, sensitivity and understanding need to be demonstrated in certain instances. There is no better example of this than the case of Mary Lamb, sister of the writer Charles Lamb.

On the evening of 21 September 1796, Mary developed symptoms of mania and a doctor was called. He could not be found, and later, as E V Lucas wrote: 'For a few dreadful moments his sister's reason utterly left her and in a paroxysm of rage she stabbed her mother to

COMMITTEE ON INSANITY AND CRIME,

REPORT

OF THE

Committee appointed to consider what changes, if any, are
desirable in the existing law, practice and procedure
relating to criminal trials in which the plea of insanity
as a defence is raised, and whether any and, if so,
what changes should be made in the existing
law and practice in respect of cases falling
within the provisions of section 2 (4)
of the Criminal Lunatics Act, 1884,

Presented to Parliament by Command of His Majesty.

LONDON:

PRINTED & PUBLISHED BY HIS MAJESTY'S STATIONERY OFFICE.
To be purchased directly from H.M. STATIONERY OFFICE at the following addresses:
Imperial House, Kingsway, London, W.C.2; 28, Abingdon Street, London, S.W.1;
York Street, Manchester; 1, St. Andrew's Crescent, Cardiff;
or 120, George Street, Edinburgh;
or through any Bookseller.

1924

Price 6d. net.

A Report of the Committee on Insanity and Crime, 1924. Author's collection

the heart.' There was a coroner's inquest and in the report we have this: 'It seems the young lady had once before, in her earlier years, been deranged from the harassing fatigues of too much business. As her carriage towards her mother was always affectionate in the extreme... it is to be attributed to the present insanity of this ill-fated young woman.' She was committed to the 'Islington madhouse' as it was then called, but later came back into normal life, with her brother as nurse for the rest of her life.

In court cases for murder, the idea of diminished responsibility took a very long time to be established. In 1949 there was prolonged discussion on this, with the focus on the use and importance of medical witnesses. Sir Theobald Matthew stated that, 'I know there are a number of persons in Broadmoor as a result of special verdicts who have never been certified and who are not considered by the superintendent as being certifiable.'

In 1957 the case of Francis Harrison demonstrated the common problems of the notion. He had murdered his wife, striking her on the head with an axe; the judge rejected a manslaughter submission on the grounds of diminished responsibility. The judge, Mr Justice Diplock, retained the murder decision, saying: 'This was not a motiveless crime... what the jury had to decide was whether Harrison's hysterical personality was of such a kind... as to amount to something more than mere lack of control...' He was given life imprisonment.

Chapter 2

OTHER CRIMES AGAINST THE PERSON

ASSAULTS

An assault is 'any act committed intentionally or recklessly, which leads another person to fear immediate personal violence. This becomes battery if force is applied without consent. Again, the Offences Against the Persons Act of 1861 consolidated this into the category of offences which had penalties lessened unless they were 'aggravated' – had a more serious factor involved.

It is obvious from these definitions that all kinds of altercations, brawls and disagreements in the common course of life were destined to be examined in the law courts. A trawl of the magistrates' courts and assize courts once again provides an insight into the range of offences under this heading. Before the 1820s, and since the early 1700s, it had been a capital offence. The source of this savage and extreme lawmaking is the so-called 'Bloody Code.' The death penalty was extended in a statute of 1688 and a succession of murder acts increased the number of capital offences. Because by the mid eighteenth century there was much more need to preserve property, as capitalistic culture increased, a large number of offences against both property and person came along. As James Sharpe has written: 'By 1750 the criminal law was primarily the bulwark of property.' But later in that century and in the Regency period, there was an increasing number of highway robberies; the phenomenon of the highwayman accelerated after the last years of the seventeenth century, and footpads were always a danger. With the wars with France and Napoleon from the 1790s to 1815 and after, there were increasing numbers of deserters, beggars and desperate poor on the roads, providing a source of serious assault to travelers.

But assault was not a hanging offence – it was dealt with in a

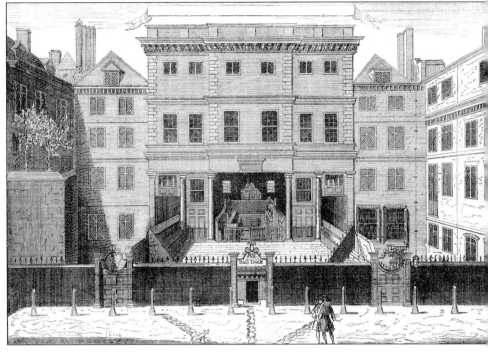

The Old Bailey Sessions House c.1750. Author's collection

variety of ways. Often the result was a discharge, a fine for damages or a spell in gaol.

The toughness of the criminal justice system in the early eighteenth century is encapsulated in this brief summary of the Old Bailey sessions printed in the *Annual Register* in 1732:

The sessions ended at the Old Bailey when 7 malefactors received sentence of death, viz. Thomas Beck and Peter Robinson, for the high-way; Dorothy Fosset for stealing two guineas from a person in drink; Richard Wentland for a street robbery; Anne Wentland his wife for forcibly taking from Henry Parker £10... Hurst was held up at the bar top receive sentence, and died on the back of one who was carrying him to the cells. The 2 women pleaded their bellies, Wentland only was found pregnant; 25 ordered for transportation, 3 burnt in the hand, and 4 to be whipped.

This incident is typical of thousands such assaults in what is termed 'the long eighteenth century': in the Blue Pig tavern in 1788 Mr Greenall was enjoying some time in the pub and was sober, whereas a man called Parker had been drinking for hours. In court, it was said that without the least provocation, Parker came up to Greenall and said, 'Are you there, bungy-nosed bob?' He then struck him hard on the temple and then hit him again. The two men were old friends and used to spar together, so this might have seemed normal to some, but it went to court and Greenall won. It should never really have gone to court, and Greenall was awarded one shilling.

In contrast, in the 1804 Guildhall sessions in the City of London, a variety of assault occurred in trial known as 'cutting and maiming' and at times that was an offence leading to transportation. On this occasion, John Johnson cut and maimed one Charles Higgs. He had stuck a knife in the victim's cheek bone with such force that it was a considerable time before it could be withdrawn.' Johnson was given a two-year gaol sentence.

This shows that the general term assault covered a wide range of matters. But not so many average cases of assault (that is from brawls) ended in prison. The anonymous author of *Old Bailey Experience*, published in 1833, listed 'the principal actors in criminality' as evident behind bars there in sixteen main crimes, and only two of these were violent: highwaymen and 'women and men who waylay inebriate persons...'

BODILY HARM

Under the 1861 act referred to above, the distinction was made between actual and grievous bodily harm. Actual was 'an assault causing actual bodily harm' and grievous was done 'maliciously or with intent – serious injury short of death.' This latter was, naturally, an indictable offence. In the assize courts and later in courts of appeal, there is ample documentation and in the first years of work in the courts after 1861, it is clear that there were some difficulties in distinguishing the two terms.

What is important to grasp is how violent assault was differently treated as time went on. Historian Martin Wiener sums this up: 'By the opening of Victoria's reign the transition from 'civil' to 'criminal' treatment of assault was almost complete.

Within the criminal courts that handled assault – petty and quarter sessions – the hitherto usual practice of dropping assault charges upon reconciliation or imposing a nominal fine upon some kind of compensation to the complainant were increasingly subject to criticism by magistrates, and giving way to the imposition of some kind of prison sentence.'

RESEARCH PROCESS

The location of records and sources for violent crime are many and varied, but the focus is on all criminal courts after 1861, and before that, mainly on petty and quarter sessions. But it has to be recalled that church courts also provide sources. For instance, in the Lincolnshire village of North Kelsey in 1892 the vicar, the Reverend Curry, set about the schoolmaster, Mr Ralphs, actually in the classroom, in front of the children. Ralphs had been allowed to have a school photograph taken, with permission from the School Board. But this was the last thing that Curry was going to allow on that fateful day. The vicar bolted the door and commanded all to stay where they were. Curry leapt across the room and grabbed the schoolmaster, putting his arm in a grip. Then he chased him after he broke free, and took him by the throat. The children ran away.

The case could have been heard in the consistory court, prosecuted by the National Union of Elementary Teachers. But charges were dropped. Ironically, it was in that year that the Clergy Discipline Act was passed, stating that internal affairs within the church would be dealt with by the Bishop. In 1904, a vicar from Carrington was defrocked by that process, but that was for a sexual misdemeanour.

This shows that for assaults of various kinds, the research span goes further than the criminal courts. Various church courts need to be distinguished, and they will be good sources for other offences, in later chapters, but it has to be mentioned here that church courts go back to the tenth century, and traditionally the Bishop in each area would make visitations at first yearly and then triennially; there were also archdeacons' courts. The consistory court was the Bishop's own. Cases were known as causes, and so for research purposes the historian needs to look for act or court books, and to look at causes. There were five types of causes and not all of these would concern crime history, but those that do have a place here are:

Defamation (see more in Chapter 7)

Matrimonial (these may involve assaults)

Officium Dominum (Office of the Judge) This would include mostly moral issues (Chapter 7) but cases such as that of North Kelsey were not uncommon – including fights over designated church pews.

CASE STUDIES

Actual Bodily harm

In 1863, Thomas Ireland and Henry Spencer appeared at the Middlesex sessions for unlawfully assaulting Benjamin Hower. Hower was supervising the two men, who worked as drovers for his master and had been dismissed. Hower's task was to check they stole nothing. But he was knocked unconscious by Ireland and had a severe nosebleed for hours after. A witness stated that the two men had stolen items from a chest. Other witnesses told a tale of extreme violence, as a constable came to arrest them and then he in turn was threatened and attacked. He was kicked and his ear cut. The injuries amounted to actual bodily harm at first on indictment, but then it was re-expressed as grievous bodily harm. The sentence was eighteen months' hard labour.

A more clear-cut case was that of three men who assaulted Matthew Goff in 1862. They were shown to have intent to murder, disable and do grievous bodily harm. These were three poachers who had attacked a gamekeeper, attempting to throttle him with a scarf. The sentence was fifteen months' hard labour for the main culprit.

Chapter 3

SOCIAL PROTEST

PUBLIC ORDER AND RIOTS/MUTINY

British history is packed with public disorder and there are whole libraries on the major rebellions such as the Peasants' Revolt or the Pilgrimage of Grace. But what about the more mundane riots and demonstrations – the ones your ancestors are far more likely to have been involved in – and to have been arrested? In the course of time, riots happened over food prices, perceived injustice, objections to the militia being sent in to sort out local trouble, political radicalism and of course strike activity during the years of the growth of trade unionism as legal entities and later when matters were more universally unstable as in the General Strike of 1926.

In limited space, we can only summarise some of these here, but the starting point is in the famous 'Riot Act' – the source of the word riot is in this definition: 'A riot is an unlawful assembly which has begun to execute its common purpose by a breach of the peace and to the terror of the public.' Unlawful assembly and riots are misdemeanours, punishable by fines and imprisonment. The Act of 1715 said that if twelve persons or more are gathered unlawfully, tumultuously gathered together for more than an hour after the reading of the Riot Act, then they were guilty of a felony and they could incur a maximum penalty of penal servitude for life.

A quick way to grasp the enormity of that law as applied at various times is to look at the treatment of the Chartist radicals in the 1830s and 1840s: many were imprisoned as common criminals, for no more than speaking openly about parliamentary reform. Equally, a look at the fight for trade union legality shows similar repression. In 1799 and 1800 the Combination Acts prevented gatherings of more than six people in a public thoroughfare.

A mutiny was something else, but a related concept. Mutiny as a crime is best explained by reference to the 1688 Bill of Rights which refers to the illegality of a person keeping a standing army, but the notion of mutiny was of course most threatening in terms of war, and the famous naval mutinies at the Nore and at Spithead in the 1790s exemplify the magnitude of the offence when the state is at war.

Less exalted cases are typified by the trials at Admiralty sessions (often at the Old Bailey). In 1811 for instance, Thomas O'Hara was executed for mutiny at Sheerness. He had run away with a prize brig and had gone into enemy service. The sentence was death. But in many trials over the course of the early nineteenth century in particular, indictments for mutiny failed, because there was so much cruelty, inequality and injustice in the lives of seamen. For passenger ships when mutiny was charged, there were often plenty of civilian witnesses and the accused were often acquitted.

RADICALISM AND POLITICAL MOVEMENTS

The years c.1790-1840 were decades of social unrest on a large scale in Britain. The industrial revolution and the mass movements of labour through immigration and movements from country to town meant that there was an increase in the demand for political and social change; the extremes of wealth and poverty were everywhere visible and when protests were made they were suppressed with barbarity and violence, as in the Peterloo Massacre of 1819 when a peaceable gathering of people to hear Henry Hunt speak led to a charge of hussars and the slaughter of ordinary people. The year 1812 was particularly extreme in this sense, and the story of the Luddites in Yorkshire in that year illustrate the criminal law in relation to social unrest.

The Luddites in this case were the shearsmen in the clothing industry of the West Riding and they were so organized and numerous that they conducted a reign of terror in the factories around them. It took the army and the creation of a new offence to catch and charge them: the taking of an unlawful oath, which was a capital offence, and nineteen of these workers were hanged at York.

Chartism was a threat to social order in many places as the campaign to extend the franchise grew, and the early 1830s were the years of violence and fear in the eastern counties in rural locations, as the so-called Captain Swing agricultural wave of crime accelerated. Punishment of offenders in these cases was swift and merciless and the assizes are full of cases of death sentences for arson, sheep-stealing and robbery, but many of these were spin-offs from the crowd crime of the poor and dispossessed.

The paperchase through the courts in these cases range from magistrates' courts to the Old Bailey, but the documentation is very substantial so any Chartist or Luddite ancestors should not be hard to trace. Jeremy Irons, in one of the first television programmes in the *Who Do You Think You Are* series, discovered a London Chartist in his family tree. The events were widely reported in the press.

RESEARCH PROCESS
Riots
For riots – over corn prices, police brutality or even, as often happened, over the presence of an unpopular public figure or even at a hanging – the press reports are voluminous. As ever, the journalists liked a good crowd fight and a confrontation between groups. There are also many cases of riots caused by racist attitudes, such as seeing Irish immigrants as scapegoats for crime (which often happened in Liverpool, Manchester and Bradford where Irish immigration was widespread).

Of course, riots and disorder almost always led to other crimes, as one of the following case studies shows. If ancestors were arrested in these contexts, then they will be found in the court records (various petty sessions usually) and also in the prison records in many cases.

Mutiny
Cases of mutiny may be found in the press reports, and in the records of the admiralty courts. They will appear in courts-martial as well as in admiralty court records. It has to be said that, as press reports show, in many cases, justice was summarily done, offenders being shot.

CASE STUDIES
Riot
Eliza, fifty years old, was Mr Chorley's cook and when she roasted a joint for him, she expected the dripping to take home. Chorley was a powerful man in the city: a magistrate and also a respected surgeon. But respect went out of the door on this occasion. It was when she was sent to Armley Gaol for the offence of taking the dripping that the trouble started. She was convicted of stealing two

pounds of the stuff and given one month's imprisonment.

She was quite new to his employment, having been there for only a few months, living in. When challenged about the matter she said that she was allowed it 'as a perquisite though I said nothing about that perquisite when I was first engaged to do the work'.

All hell broke out around Chorley's place. What had happened to make things worse was that her trial had been held in camera, and the Mayor of Leeds himself had been on the bench. The spark was lit, so to speak, by an article in a paper, as a report at the time noted:

> In a few days after the committal of the woman attention was called to the case, in a spirit of indignation, by one of the local papers which is best known for its publication of sensational stories and in its indulgence of caricature sketches of local personages …

The report also noted that newsboys were shouting out scraps of gossip and jokes, and that people were chatting about the affair in disgust; in the street this rhyme was heard:

> Now all you cooks and servant girls wot's very fond of tipping
> Don't take your master's scraps of fat and boil 'em down for dripping:
> For if you do bear this in mind, the magistrates won't fail
> To try you in a private court and send you off to gaol.

Time passed and then graffiti appeared on the walls of the Chorley home and on plenty of other walls, with such words as

'A month's imprisonment for 2lbs of dripping.' Then things escalated so that Chorley was vilified in the street and indeed harassed and bullied. He received threatening letters, and then placards began to appear expressing the view that Leeds people should assemble for a large celebration when Mrs Stafford came out of prison.

But before that, pressure mounted. A large and aggressive crowd gathered outside Chorley's house. At first they shouted insults, and then they threw missiles at the house, including snowballs and stones. Chorley had the courage to come out and face them; he tried to talk to them and explain his position on the matter but to no avail.

They threw dirt at him. When the police arrived they gradually dispersed, but there was worse to come.

Late in the evening on 22 February, a huge crowd assembled outside Armley Gaol expecting Mrs Stafford to appear, but she did not. The mob expected celebration but instead found that their friend was still locked up, or so they thought. In fact she had been let out earlier. After that the crowd were determined to go again to Chorley's house and this time they contrived to hang a bottle and an old dripping-pan to the end of a long pole. The police who stood by took a very long time to move the mob away.

Still the Leeds populace were not satisfied. The next day stones were thrown at the Chorleys' windows and the mob were pressing heavily on the forces of law. To make matters worse, the Chief Constable, Mr Bell, while trying to help move the crowd, fell heavily and dislocated a shoulder. The crowd mentality took over and when people fell they were crushed and trampled. One man was under the feet of the mob and was so seriously injured he had to be taken to the infirmary. The police could not cope.

The Army at York were called for by telegraph, so by the evening men from the 8th Hussars were in Leeds and the authorities were not finished yet, because extra police from Bradford were called for as well. By 1865 the railways were well established and the soldiers travelled by train from York. There was a feeling of the riot being calmed by the time that the local journalists posted their reports but late that night a crowd of about 2,000 gathered outside the town hall and shouted out insults. The police took the brunt of the anger and as this mob was moved away, a stone cut deeply into the temple of one officer. There were several arrests, and that was inevitable given the scale of destruction and lawlessness that had filled the city like a rising tide of rage.

All this time, Mrs Stafford had been elsewhere. She had left Leeds much earlier, going to Scarborough where her daughter lived. The Times man reflected that she showed good sense 'preferring to avoid the questionable honours the crowd intended to confer upon her'. In other words, her appearance before her supporters would either have intensified the anger or made her a local hero. The politic action smacks of a reaction to sound advice from the police and prison governor. In the end, it was decided that the five men arrested should not be dealt with seriously. There was perhaps a feeling of regret for the mean and thoughtless use of power by a bench of three influential men of high status, with one woman in front of them and the Chorleys and other witnesses trailing into the town hall to condemn her. The newspapers had imagined and recreated that scene in the eyes of the public, and the formula was one for extreme disorder on the streets of Leeds.

We have to remember that the workers were one thing but the so-called 'underclass' were another matter. Usually when disorder hit the streets it was the lowest social order, desperate and pushed to the end of their tether by economic pressures such as the price of bread or the lack of jobs. But the Leeds dripping riots were, as far as we can gather, events in which decent people were goaded into militancy and sheer rage because of a terrible injustice against a decent working woman. In simple terms, it was a case of a confrontation between, on the one hand the practice of goodwill and convention ('perks of the job') and on the other hand the letter of the law.

There was an element of absolute disgust at the immorality and injustice being shown by a man in high position. With hindsight, it is possible to say that the results of the street violence were partly a continuation of the old social convention of 'rough music' when a local wrongdoer was subject to torment and bullying for a moral 'crime' and also it was a case of total callousness on the part of a man who should have known better.

Luddites

In 1812, the clothing industry of the West Riding faced the implications of the arrival of new machinery in the finishing processes of clothing manufacture: many of them did so with a resolve to fight the mechanisation. What some of them did in that zeal to survive was bring a reign of terror to villages and mills from the Pennines to the Halifax and Bradford areas. In order to defeat them, the forces of law had to bring in the militia, such was the fear across the county. The year 1812 was a time of particularly strained and repressive economic measures and poorer families were suffering. It might seem strange to mention that many of the Luddites were quite well off, but they feared the future and they did not stand idly by while the greater macroeconomic factors crushed them.

THE TRIAL

OF

FEARGUS O'CONNOR, ESQ.,

(BARRISTER-AT-LAW,)

AND FIFTY-EIGHT OTHERS,

AT LANCASTER,

ON A

CHARGE OF SEDITION, CONSPIRACY, TUMULT, AND RIOT.

MANCHESTER:
ABEL HEYWOOD, 58, OLDHAM-STREET.
LONDON:
JOHN CLEAVE, 1, SHOE-LANE, FLEET-STREET,
AND ALL BOOKSELLERS AND NEWS-VENDERS IN TOWN AND COUNTRY.

1843.

A publication reporting on a famous Chartist trial. Author's collection

They took their name from a fabled character called Ned Ludd who reputedly led similar machine-wrecking attacks in Nottingham. But arguably, a leader came on the scene in the Spen Valley who was to conduct a campaign of profound fear-instilling aggression against those employers who had new machinery installed. The focus for the campaign was the trade linked to the cloth finishing processes, in particular the shearers, of whom Mellor was one. This was a skilled business, demanding the expert use of large and unwieldy shears for trimming and finishing.

Mellor realised that the essence of success in these attacks was secrecy, because the communities along the valleys where the clothing industry flourished would all know each other well from communal occasions. He therefore had his men black their faces and always wear hats; they would then attack by night. The reign of terror lasted for some time and the local magistrates were at a loss what to do, but the chain of command broadened and the reaction of the authorities spread from the West Riding to the militia, and then to the Lord Lieutenant of the county at Wentworth Woodhouse, and eventually to the Home Secretary.

After various delays which gave the Luddites the upper hand, sheer paranoia eventually led to positive action; first it was due to military successes as a brutal and repressive group of militia conducted their own reprisals, and then, with the new Home Secretary Lord Sidmouth taking place at the Home Office, the establishment began to create an equal measure of fear in the Luddites. Soon it was a case of the magistrates finding men willing to find information, and Sidmouth was keen on the use of spies functioning as agents provocateurs.

Matters were made worse as deaths occurred: notably, there had been a murder of a factory-owner called Horsfall and Mellor, along with William Thorpe and Thomas Smith, was charged. Horsfall had been attacked on the road, shot by men positioned alongside in undergrowth. Witnesses came forward to implicate Mellor, a man who had also been pointed at by a particular turncoat and petty thief from the village of Flockton. These three men were convicted of murder and found guilty. One commentator writing in the 1830s wrote: 'It is impossible to read the details of this and the other Luddite cases without shuddering at the cold-hearted and systematic manner in which the murders were debated and agreed on...'

Mellor, Smith and Thorpe were hanged on 8 January 1813. They were led to the scaffold still in their irons; they all went down on their knees after the chaplain asked them to pray. Mellor said, 'Some of my enemies may be here. If they be, I freely forgive them, and all the world, and I hope the world will forgive me.' The bodies were taken to York County Hospital for dissection.

On 16 January, fourteen men were hanged on the conviction of taking an illegal oath and the destruction of a mill; in addition, there was a charge of riot, of course. Eight men were found guilty of riot and destruction at Cartwright's Mill, the story featuring in Charlotte

Bronte's novel, *Shirley*. There were attempts to provide alibis when several defence witnesses were called, but all that failed, and it took the jury just five minutes to decide on a guilty verdict. As was noted by several historians in earlier times, all the men were married and all left young children fatherless. The word 'Luddite' entered the language, such was the impact of that year of terror when the middle classes in the valleys of the West Riding could not sleep easily in their beds.

Mutiny

In 1825 the *Liverpool Courier* reported on two seamen called Hastings and Moharg, who were convicted of mutiny on board the Havannah. The sentence of death was passed at the admiralty sessions; the importance of this for research is that there was pressure for reprieves. No less a person than the ill-fated William Huskisson, who was to die under a train at the opening of the Liverpool-Manchester Railway a few years later, wrote to the paper to state that there had been a Royal pardon. Then Sir Robert Peel wrote also and said, 'I think it right to add that mercy has been extended in this case on account of extraordinary circumstances... which appear to His Majesty's advisers to warrant a mitigation of the punishment which... Must have been inflicted upon the parties guilty of so serious an offence as mutiny...'

Chapter 4
THEFT AND ROBBERY

ROBBERY AND HIGHWAY ROBBERY

These offences were tightly defined, and in some trials there was argument and discussion in court regarding exactly where a crime took place, because the location could mean the difference between life and death. Robbery has always been theft with force; highway robbery takes place on a recognized thoroughfare and on 'The King's highway.' If a person attacked and robbed the victim on a street then they might say it was actually in a yard then they might try to argue that they were actually on a 'highway' but often that was of course a desperate attempt to save the accused's neck in the years when the capital crimes were over 200 and highway robbery was high on that list.

Of course, Dick Turpin, Claude Duval and William Nevison ('Swift Nick') have generated stories which have created a myth of glamour

Highway robbery, from York Castle (1829). Author's collection

and drama in the lives of highwaymen, but the reality was very different. 'Highway robbery' referred mainly to footpads – desperate characters who would waylay rich men riding home from market or from the pub. There were felons who specialized in this, staying in hostelries to watch for potential victims and then following them home to attack and rob in the cover of night.

GRAND LARCENY AND LARCENY

Theft was, as B J Davey has written in his study of crime in eighteenth -century Lincolnshire, the second most common offence, with 450 cases between 1740 and 1780 in Lindsey alone. Davey writes: 'Of the 450 accused of theft, 276 went to trial; 160 were convicted and 116 acquitted.' Larceny or petty theft would be dealt with in the summary courts, but until the Theft Act of 1968 we had the crimes of larceny and grand larceny. This distinction was very important in the years of the Bloody Code because a statute of 1275 established that grand larceny referred to a theft of a certain value.

Hence, in c.1800, a thief who stole more than twelve pence had committed a capital crime. It was a common habit for courts to lower the stated value of goods to below twelve pence so that a neck would be spared. Between 1814 and 1834 there were 3,000 crimes of grand larceny merely from breaking into a dwelling house recorded and even then only forty-five of these felons were hanged.

The 1916 Larceny Act consolidated all kinds of theft in common law and statute law and listed and described virtually all potential situations and objects related to acts of theft. In 1951, Anthony Martienssen wrote: 'Larcenies and frauds are the commonest crimes, and the greater part of a detective's time is spent in catching thieves. Of the 461,000 indictable offences committed in England and Wales in 1950, 334,000 were larcenies and frauds of which 146,000 cases, or 43.5% were cleared up by the police.' Larceny is, of all crimes, the one that appeals as something offering an easy way of life, and of course it is a simple matter for the first time offender.

THEFT

This is the dishonest appropriation of property and relates to the concept of larceny in earlier writings as a generic term. In other words, in the actual writings related to the history of crime, there is a whole vocabulary within acts of theft, linking to slang and to police

J Dunn, convicted of theft. East Riding of Yorkshire Archives

usage, and even to the legal language of the courts. These will be dealt with in other chapters – for instance the theft of animals in Chapter 5. The terminology of theft in c.1800 for instance, includes these categories:
Pickpockets
Shoplifters
Snatchers from reticules
Horse and cattle stealers
Receivers of stolen goods
Stealing from carts and carriages

RESEARCH PROCESS
For all types of theft, including the related serious crimes of sheep stealing, horse stealing and cattle maiming (all capital under the Bloody Code) the petty session and assize court records, together with press reports, are valuable. In the mid nineteenth century there were also other writings, of journalists and documentarists also, whose work can add to these. Later, courts of appeal will continue the story, and of course, prison records. There will also be plenty of material in police records and in transportation records (up to 1867).

Police records are particularly useful, because the calendars of prisoners, charge books and station journals will all list such petty crimes and give all essential information.

An excellent resource for a first search is the now online Nineteenth Century British Periodicals, a service offered by the British Library.

CASE STUDIES
Highway Robbery

This is the story a man who could have been a successful farmer, had he stayed on the right side of the law. Broughton had a farm bought for him at Marton, near Sleaford, when he was just twenty-two. He also gathered more wealth when he married a woman who brought money with her, but all this was not enough for this bad seed, a man who was, in the words of his time, a rake and a villain. He began by gambling, and he mixed with bad company, including a certain John Oxley.

With Oxley, contact started with a London fence called Shaw, and soon Broughton and his friend were taking on robberies. They were paid to rob the Rotherham mail, and the two men got to Chesterfield, from where they would begin the attack. Not far from Rotherham, the two men stopped the coach and there was only the post-boy driving; he was tied up and left. The robbers took the bag but there was little worth having – merely on bill of exchange, though that was for a large sum.

While Broughton stayed in Mansfield, Oxley went to London with the bill. His problem was to convert it into money. In London, with the help of Shaw who had set up the job, Oxley saw that it was possible to do the business and walk out with the cash, in this case from a company in Austin Friars. After giving Broughton just £10 initially, Oxley found himself at the point of being pressured for more, and it seems that Broughton was pleased to take another £40.

Of course, now that the two men had come across a simple means of stealing funds, they were out on the road again; they robbed the Cambridge mail this time, and their difficulties began because a provincial bank note was traced – one of a number that the two men had been working hard to spend in order not to be traced. But they were traced after the energetic and sharp activities of a shop-boy. Some Bow Street officers traced the lodgings where Broughton was staying and, after a chase, they cornered him at an inn called The Dog and Duck. Broughton was taken to Bow Street. Their London contact Shaw turned King's evidence and he told the whole story of the robbery at Cambridge and of where and how they had dealt with and hidden the takings.

Later, the two men were examined again, and although the post-boy could not identify them, they were remanded in custody. The enterprising and wily Oxley managed to escape from Clerkenwell bridewell; he disappeared into the night and we know nothing more of him. But Broughton was taken north to York. He was tried before Mr Justice Buller at the Spring Assizes in 1792. There was Shaw against him again, and also a man called Close who had assisted in the financial transactions in London. Broughton was told by the judge that there was not 'a shadow of hope' of any mercy.

Spence Broughton was to be hanged, and also gibbeted. He was reported as having faced that sentence with fortitude, and he prepared himself for death, and was reportedly what the authorities would have called 'a model prisoner'. He died with four others on 14 April 1792, and before he expired said, 'This is the happiest day that I have experienced for some time.' The story of Broughton does not end there, however. His body was gibbeted on Attercliffe Common, not far from the Arrow Inn and there was a weekend like a local feast day, with his body being pulleyed up into position on the Monday morning. But some years later, in 1827, a man called Sorby bought the land around the gibbet, and a few years before that, when some of the bones of the highwayman had loosened and fallen, the tale is told of a local potter who took some of the skeleton's fingers and used them to make some bone china items. One of these, a jug, was sold in London in 1871. Such is the notoriety of this Sheffield rogue that over the years, people have horded and preserved anything related to his story, and in one of the York archive stores, a piece of the gibbet is still preserved.

Grand Larceny

At the Old Bailey in 1807, Benjamin Hanfield was convicted of grand larceny, but he had also committed a murder, and for the theft he was sentenced to be transported for seven years. In this record we have a concise summary of his processing in the system because he confessed to the murder:

It appeared that Hanfield, a considerable time subsequent to the

Baron Rolfe, who sentenced many felons to die.
Author's collection

murder, was convicted at the Old Bailey of grand larceny and sentenced to seven years transportation. He was conveyed on board a hulk at Woolwich to await his conveyance to New South Wales, and having suddenly been taken with a severe illness, and tortured in his mind by a recollection of the murder, about which he raved, he said he wished to make a discovery (confession) before he died. A message was sent to the police magistrates and an officer was sent to bring him before them. They sent him, in the custody of an officer, to Hounslow Heath, when he pointed out the fatal spot where the murder was perpetrated.

Sometimes, matters were much simpler, as when James Blackburn was sentenced to six months hard labour in the Aylsham bridewell for breaking into a house and stealing two legs of pork.

Larceny

This was everyday stuff for the magistrates across the land. In a busy day at the Old Bailey, in December 1787, William Read was charged with larceny after being caught stealing lead from a building in the

Maggie Smith, an habitual offender. East Riding Archives

Circus, Marylebone; Ann Brooks was taken 'with three sheets upon her' and was guilty of larceny but cleared of burglary, and Hannah Peeling also, for stealing a watch and running into a house, where she was cornered and arrested.

Burglary
Burglary is entering a building with intent to steal, or entering a building and stealing items – or inflicting bodily harm on any person while in that act. Two hundred and thirty-three were hanged for the offence between 1814 and 1834.

Three burglars were hanged at Lincoln in 1784. Thomas Wood broke into a house at Saxilby and stole a silver tankard and some money. He had done the job with some accomplices who had not been traced; the housewife had been disturbed by the noise and she woke to find Wood in the house, and the burglar threatened her and her husband with violence. After the villains' escape, it took only a week to trace them and they were arrested.

Downind and Davison stole similar objects and cash from a house in Langrick Ferry. Their haul included the very large sum of £20. But it was the old story of the thieves being caught trying to sell the stolen goods that brought them down; they tried to sell the booty in Boston. Long and tall tales were given about supposed other men burying goods, but all to no avail.

They were all in court before Baron Eyre on 10 March. What made things much worse for the felons was that Richard Bull (a robber) and Davison had tried to escape some weeks before the trial. There was no question of mercy after that, even though Davison had a pregnant wife. This is a particularly interesting case because there is a printed broadsheet giving details of the hangings. Many of these have not survived, as they were ephemeral printings, but we know from this that 'they mounted the steps with great fortitude, acknowledged themselves guilty of the crimes for which they suffered and begged the spectators to be warned by their untimely end.' There was also a rare episode of drama when two young men who had been reprieved after trial for horse-stealing actually walked up to place the ropes and caps on the condemned. This was an extra piece of ritual, not often performed, in which the nature of a reprieve was highlighted for all present. We read that '... the young men descended and the trembling offenders, calling upon the Saviour of the World to receive them... left suspended by the neck until they were dead.'

Theft

This was, as the foregoing discussion makes clear, a generic term and is used in that way in reports, as in this from the Old Bailey in 1785:

> Stairs Stroud and George Clayton were tried for stealing some chains, the property of a Mr Scott. No-one saw the prisoners commit the theft, but some time after the chains had been missed, they were found with Stroud...guilty.

Chapter 5

RURAL CRIME:
GAME, ANIMALS, ARSON
AND POACHING

PROPERTY AND FEAR

As the commercial imperative drove social change in Britain, most markedly from the last years of the sixteenth century when the East India Company was founded and the new American colonies were about to be opened out, the centrality of property and ownership of material wealth became universal. The inevitable development of the haves and have-nots was to bring with it all the legal and criminal issues associated with such a situation. The early eighteenth century consolidated this, as the British Empire took shape more prominently and the wealth at home gathered by investors led to the building of country houses, estates, landscaping, deer parks and the culture of hunting, shooting and fishing.

There was then the Industrial Revolution and the more widespread creation of enclosure, with more and more common land being taken in; in the war period of 1792-1815, Parliament assented to 956 bills of enclosure. The poor suffered terribly; as historians have often pointed out, the damage done to rural communities was both material and moral. Of course, crime and deprivation go hand in hand.

THE CONCEPT OF SOCIAL CRIME

In such extreme circumstances, the notion of common land and food sources being open to all, there was a certain credence given to what was later the campaign ideology of Proudhon the French socialist, that 'property is theft'. In other words, if there were game birds and rabbits both accessible and plentiful, surely a poor family man could feed his family with their flesh? At the centre of this was the ancient craft of poaching and it attendant culture. This gave rise to the trade of gamekeeper, and thus began the land wars, going on all the time

The Beverley Arms and court. Here Dick Turpin was first arraigned. The author

like a cat and mouse game, with its own rituals and rules. When that code was broken, and a poacher shot dead a keeper, the punishment was extreme and merciless.

THE BLOODY CODE

As has been previously summarised, a succession of repressive 'murder acts' in the century after the 1688 rebellion, gradually assembled hundreds of capital crimes. The Game Laws were prominent in this; those of 1684 concerned the taking of game by anyone other than persons who owned a freehold estate of at least £100 per annum, or who were the son and heir apparent of a person of a higher degree. In 1723 the 'Black Act' made many kinds of poaching into felonies, and there were other repressive acts, up to 1816. An indication of the severity of the regime in the first fifty years of the eighteenth century is that between 1700 and 1750 in London and Middlesex, there were just over 3,000 capital convictions and 1,714 executions. There was also the hiatus between the loss of America and the new use of Australia as a destination for felons. This period meant that it was perhaps easier to hang than to fill the gaols to a point of crisis.

POACHING AND STEALING ANIMALS

The spirit behind such famous folk songs as *The Lincolnshire Poacher* expresses much of the popular mediation of what was for some a sport and for others the only activity that kept away starvation in the family. As poaching offences were tried largely at a magistrates' court in the first instance, there would be local knowledge and a certain degree of leniency and human understanding, as with sheep-stealing also, but in the statutes such offences as robbing warrens, being armed and disguised in a forest, stealing any fish from a river or pond, and breaking down the head or mound of a fish pond were capital offences.

Sheep stealing is an interesting case. In many English counties, a desperate man could easily steal a sheep and feed his whole family. But there are numerous cases in which people were clearly making a large-scale business out of stealing sheep, so repression was severe. James Huntingdon stole three sheep in 1784 and was hanged for it. William Teer stole three fleeces of hog wool and a hempen sack and was transported for seven years in 1795. William Crow, in the same year, stole a milk cow and was hanged.

Horse-stealing was common throughout the seventeenth and eighteenth centuries (it was Dick Turpin's main trade). The theft of a mare could easily mean fourteen years in Van Dieman's Land; it was common practice to hang convicted felons for most animal thefts in the years c.1790-1830.

RESEARCH PROCESS

Quarter Sessions records and press reports are again good sources here. The early nineteenth century was the age of societies for the prosecution of felons, and so there are quite full accounts of prosecutions resulting from actions by those bodies. Trial transcripts are obtained at the Old Bailey sessions online (see Bibliography). But the best sources are at the county record office in the quarter sessions reports. Usually, information is brief, but if there are other crimes, such as assaults and bodily harm or even murder, emerging from what was intended to be a poaching expedition, then a substantial narrative comes through into the reports and into the press.

It is important to remember that the location of the sessions hearings will be listed in the archives' index, so a careful study of those lists is the first step, otherwise time will be wasted. A good ordnance survey map of the period in question is extremely useful too. In Lincolnshire, for instance, there were quarter sessions in the areas of Lindsey, Holland and Kesteven, the ancient demarcations of the county's divisions.

CASE STUDIES
Poaching
Regular quarter session business

At the quarter sessions in Chelmsford, five 'well known characters' were convicted of poaching 'within the last month'. Thomas Lewis, in 1816, was a hogger and poulterer and was fined £5 for buying a hare of a person 'lately convicted as a poacher'.

More dramatic

Tried at Kingston on the Home Circuit (so this was an assize hearing), Thomas Coventry had been poaching on the manor of a Mr Broadwood. He was warned off by the gamekeeper and replied, 'Go string your fiddles and don't interrupt me.' Coventry was a young man who was the son of a noble family but he had 'dissipated wealth with every kind of extravagance'. He and his friends went to cause havoc with their double-barrelled guns on land wherever they found the opportunity. The amazing result of this trial was that Coventry was given a fine of just one shilling. A man from the lower classes would have had a spell in gaol, at least.

Sheep-stealing and damage – the 1830s, crisis years

In 1831 a judge in Salisbury sent twenty-five men to be hanged. One prisoner had assaulted an officer of the parish and the others were involved in a riot. One newspaper report said that 'On the men leaving the court a most distressing scene occurred. Their wives, their mothers, their sisters, and their children clung around them and the prisoners wept like infants.' That report was typical of a decade in which fear and criminality raged across the land like a forest fire, and

Lincolnshire shuddered like every other county.

In Lincoln in the same year rioting broke out near Sawtry and spread across into Northamptonshire. What was happening became a terror across the Eastern counties and it became known as the 'Captain Swing' crime wave. These events took their name from riots that began in East Kent and spread widely, spurred by low wages and desperately poor conditions for all farm workers. Threatening letters that were sent to farmers were signed 'Captain Swing' (a reference to swinging on the gallows). Obviously, the nickname created a certain shiver of apprehension in the wealthier people and that fear extended as far as Grimsby and in particular to the areas around Waltham and Laceby where large and open villages were susceptible to such attacks and crime. The main offences were rick-burning , animal-maiming and sheep-stealing.

The men who committed the offences were running a high risk. Sheep-stealing was an offence that had sent hundreds to the gallows. But in most cases in these villages, the land was marshland pasture settled by small landholders, and of course they would be vulnerable and would look to the magistrates' courts to protect them. In one village, Bradley Haverstoe, court records have given us a detailed picture of what measures were taken to try to stop the terrifying attacks and burnings that were creating a profoundly difficult situation. Fortunately, a collection of handbills and posters issued by Skeltons the printers has also helped us to understand the measures taken, the rewards and indeed the nature of the fears among the landed classes.

Records from the Petty Sessions survive; these were meetings at which magistrates would gather with solicitors in Grimsby and decide on punishments. William Marshall was the Grimsby man in this group, along with the solicitor Joseph Daubney, who kept the records. More serious offences would be dealt with at Quarter Sessions in larger towns, but the records of the Petty Sessions give us a valuable insight into how efforts were made to repress the villains and their activities. These records cover the years 1831 to 1840, so they give a good idea of the local echoes of the major national troubles going on as the agitation for the reform of the suffrage was developing, the Captain Swing problems and indeed the long-standing criminal issues linked with the repressive Game Acts.

There was clearly deep-seated hatred and resentment from the workers, as one offence shows: a labourer called Edward Borrell wrote a threatening letter to William Keyworth who was a local constable as well as a businessman in Laceby. Borrell was traced after sending a note in which he said, 'Firing is no warning to you at Laceby; you must not try the poor so any longer… if you do not raise their wages you must suffer by the consequence.' As a measure of just how tough the law was at that time, we have to note that Borrell was sentenced to transportation for life after his appearance at the assizes. But other offences were regular occurrences, such as horses being maimed and corn-stacks set on fire. In an effort to let solidarity do its part as well as the usual legal measures, Bradley Haverstoe created a self-help group called an Association for the Prosecution of Felons. This meant that villains would be aware that there was a sense of unity on their intended victims. So active and determined were the local traders and farmers in their efforts to protect themselves that they were alarmed by a tramp who was taken in for merely saying that 'it was a pity that more stacks were not burned'.

The really interesting clues to the fears inspired by Captain Swing and other popular revolts are in the bills printed by Skelton, and of course, in the rewards offered. For instance, £100 was the reward offered for the capture of people who had been involved in incendiarism. The bill says: 'The Committee of the Grimsby Association for the Prevention and Detection of Incendiarism offer the reward of one hundred pounds for the discovery of the person or persons who maliciously set fire to the corn-stacks of Mr Richard Faulding of Waltham…'

In 1830 a man had been executed in Lincoln for sheep-stealing and that was a common fear among the farmers of course. Their only defence was to instil fear. Poor men would naturally risk their lives when it was a question of staving off the horrors of starvation in their families. But sheep were not only stolen: they were slaughtered in acts of sheer malevolence, such was the deep hatred of the landholders. Joseph Daubney, in his capacity of secretary to the Bradley Haverstoe group, stated on one of his notices that such a horrible crime had taken place in January 1832, saying, ' … some evil disposed person or persons on Saturday night the 14th or early on Sunday morning… slaughtered a shearling wether sheep, the property of Mr William Marshall of Humberstone.'

Arson

Obviously, in farming areas, this was a real worry; often sacked labourers would set fire to stacks and outhouses in revenge, or sometimes there would be gangs at work for this, as in the 'Captain Swing' years (early 1830s). This case is typical of the problem of arson in North Yorkshire when so-called 'Wolds Rangers' were often at work. These were labourers working casually and travelling from place to place. But this is a vengeance case.

This gallows tale began with a dispute over some horses in a pinfold (the pound were stray animals were kept) at Lotherton, and involved a bitter hatred that Mary Hunter had for Mr Marshall, who had land in addition to the pinfold. Mary rowed with Marshall over a supposed four pence he owed her. The case went before a magistrate and she lost. Mary was heard to say,

'I'll be revenged if I hang for it.' There had been a fight over the affair before it was heard in court.

Mary tried all available methods to induce a servant girl called Hannah Gray to set fire to Marshall's haystacks. She threatened her and then offered money. In court, it was said that Mary promised Hannah a new frock if she would do it, and then later said she would 'tear her liver out' if she did not. At that time, there was rural crime across much of England: it was the time of the 'Captain Swing' riots and rural destruction, mainly across the Eastern counties. Animals were maimed and stacks set on fire, the trouble rooted in the deprivation suffered by farm labourers and the exploitation of poor labour by the rich landholders. Mary Hunter had allowed something of that spirit to influence her when she thought of revenge.

One question was whether or not her husband, Thomas, was involved, but he was questioned and released. Then, a few days after the first fire, three more stacks were burned. The epidemic of stack-burning also infected Ebenezer Wright, a young man who had used that crime as revenge, as Mary had; he was angry at a solicitor called Oxley at Rotherham, who had led a prosecution against him. His accomplice Norburn had turned King's evidence and expected to be released, but at first both men were tried and sentenced to hang; then Norburn was reprieved.

Finally, there was another man on the scaffold with Mary Hunter. This was Thomas Law, who had committed highway robbery when he attacked a man called Atkinson as he was returning from Pontefract market. He attacked him on the road near Ferrybridge. He inflicted twenty head-wounds on the poor man and left him for dead. But amazingly, the victim recovered and he testified against Law, who was called a 'reckless and desperate man' by the reporter for The Times. Law's most memorable words before he died were. 'May the Devil get the witnesses, they have sworn most falsely against us!'

Mary Hunter, a mother of nine children, died at York with the two men; it must have been a noisy, aggressive and unrepentant trio on view as the crowds looked on.

Chapter 6
FRAUD AND DECEPTION

UTTERING AND COUNTERFEITING

As the Bank of England (founded in 1694) and the various regional banks arrived on the financial scene and the printing of notes and production of coins from the Mint increased, there were openings for counterfeiters. The term 'uttering' was an older term for forgery. In the eighteenth century 'clipping' became something of a profitable business for criminals. Coins would be trimmed and the metal thus obtained could be used to make new coins.

With all this in mind, the commonest crimes in this category were forging coinage, producing counterfeit notes and committing frauds on cheques and bills. Some of the crimes in these categories were very major indeed – involving huge sums of money, and there is a vast secondary source literature on them. If your ancestor was a forger or fraudster, you will find plenty of material. The penalties were severe and these were largely hanging offences. In the early nineteenth century, there was a ring of counterfeiters, working a network between Warwickshire and Hull, and it is clear that such crooks took advantage of the poor communications between counties. It was up to constables and magistrates to try to pursue suspect individuals across the land, using what publications were available to offer rewards and give visual descriptions.

FORGERY

This offence is defined as a person 'making a false instrument with the intention that he, she or another shall use it to induce another to accept it as genuine'. It was common because there was general use of handwritten credit notes; fake documents were common, and the records are crammed with cases in which industrialists and other important persons were exploited in this way. The criminal simply needed a ruse of some kind in order to see a signature on a cheque, and also, as Henry Mayhew noted, forged notes were used often 'by pretended horse-dealers in fairs and markets, and at hotels by persons who pretended to be travelers'. But all this was risky up to the 1830s, because there was no mercy at the assizes for such crimes.

CONMEN AND SWINDLERS

These offenders have always been with us, but again, with the growth of urban communities and better communications, more opportunities arose for these kinds of cons. The records in the eighteenth through to the twentieth century, in courts of all kinds, offer accounts of hundreds of different scams, from the work of impostors to false claimants, begging-letter writers and crafty street-workers out to 'bilk' their victims.

Henry Mayhew's massive work of documentary, *London Labour and the London Poor* (1861-62) categorises these minutely, showing that dishonest activity was easily worked into all kinds of other 'trades' on the streets. He describes the thefts, work of 'fences' and use of children as instruments of crime, in the low lodging houses.

Naturally, there has always been speculation and insider trading, and there are famous examples of this. One of the most infamous figures was Jabez Balfour whose biography has been written by David McKie. Balfour defrauded thousands of people and ran away to Argentina, where he lived under an assumed name, but the law caught up with him. He left a trail of devastation and ruin. As McKie writes: 'Find that Jabez was £10,000 in debt to his ruined bank, the official receiver sent staff to search his apartment in Whitehall Court, where they found very little... Further enquiries ... established the overall debts of the Balfour group at more than £7 million – the equivalent of something like £450 million at the opening of the twenty-first century.'

RESEARCH PROCESS

Counterfeiting/ Uttering

These were major offences all through time, and the best sources are therefore in the assize court records, but also there were substantial reports in the press, and very much so in the national newspapers. There are also extensive primary sources from contemporary writers.

Forgery

The Bank of England archives have a wealth of material on this. That body paid agents to be vigilant on observation and checking of potential forgers. There are also petitions here from criminals in prison. A session at the archive in Freshfields Solicitors Archives has to be booked in advance, and the archives are open from 10am – 4.30pm Monday to Friday.

Fraud
The records are at TNA HO45/10022/A55279 and MEPO 2/2488. For begging-letter writers, see TNA HO45 as above. There is also the source of police records, not only in the usual charge books and calendars of prisoners, but in such places as station detective journals. It was common practice for officers to enter all kinds of character information in these journals, stating locations and movements of know criminals, or giving descriptions of fraudsters who were being pursued or investigated.

Another aspect of this is to consider the range of courts in which fraud cases might be heard. In 1828 there were trials for fraud in a Special Baronial Court for Lambeth, held at a hotel on Westminster Bridge; the Insolvent Debtors' Court, Bow Street Magistrates' Court, the Vice Chancellor's Court and the Court of Common Council the Guildhall.

If the researcher knows that a fraud was committed and the date or span of dates are known, then a search in *The Times* or Guardian Digital Archives should locate the trial. But then the actual court records could be accessed to amplify the narrative. It should be recalled also that more prominent fraud cases are often discussed in judges' memoirs and in other memoirs. There are even books available with personal memories of magistrates' courts. The London Police Court missionaries are once again useful here.

CASE STUDIES
'The Yellow Trade' – clipping
In the mid to late eighteenth century, clipping coinage in order to produce new coins from the cuttings was a popular way of literally making money. It was, naturally, a capital offence and became known as 'the yellow trade'. Arguably the most notorious gang of coiners were the Cragg Vale men in the Calder Valley. The central figure in the gang was 'King' David Hartley, and he and his associates did well for some time, until the local businessmen had enough and set about

The Old Cock, Halifax, where the 'King' of the Coiners was arrested. The author

counteracting him. In 1767 an exciseman, William Dighton, was called in to investigate. The only option open to Hartley's men was to remove Dighton from the scene. When Hartley was arrested and taken to the Old Cock Inn in Halifax, Dighton's death was looking more likely than ever.

Thomas Spencer, Robert Thomas and Matthew Normanton tried to lie in wait for Dighton twice, and failed. But on the third occasion, at

Swires Road in Halifax, Thomas and Normanton succeeded; the exciseman was shot dead. But the murder was savagely avenged; the killers were tracked down and taken to York for trial. But their bodies were put in chains on Beacon Hill, above where the railway station stands in Halifax today. If ever there was an effective deterrent it was this: the beacon can be seen for miles across the valley. The authorities at the time had to make a show of power; after all they were dealing with gangs who lived in distant, inaccessible places up into the Pennines. Any officer or official who might take them on was a courageous type indeed; and the exciseman had paid the ultimate price for that courage and enterprise.

But the story does not end there: it led to one of the most cruel murders ever recorded in Yorkshire. This happened in Heptonstall in 1771 – a village nestling up a very steep slope from the Lancashire road. Here, an informer called Abraham Ingham was cornered by a gang at the Cross Inn and was paid off most heartlessly for his blood money from the authorities. Ingham was grabbed and forced towards the open fire. The men heated some tongs and then fastened them around his neck. His head was then thrust into the flames. The gang members were yet more determined to see their victim die in agony. They dropped burning coals down his trousers. One account says that the poor man was spread-eagled over the fire and roasted to death.

Fraud

Some common examples from 1815: first, the case of Hannah Prowning, who fraudulently obtained a guinea from Thomas Weeble *The Times* report was as follows:

It appeared that a woman named Blundel belonged to a Benefit society, held at the Fountain, Broad Street, and that a short time since the prisoner attended one of these meetings, and represented that Mrs B was very ill, and much in want of money… one guinea was therefore forwarded to Mrs B… but the whole was a fraud. Mr Fielding said that the offence became aggravated by the fraud having been committed on a charitable association, and that this was a transportable offence…

At the Winchester assizes in the same year, we find ensign Henry Horton and Thomas Graham were found guilty of fraud against a

Chapter 7

OFFENCES SEXUAL AND IMMORAL

RAPE AND SEXUAL ASSAULT

Rape and sexual assault in criminal history present all kinds of difficulties for a family or social historian. It is also significant that it was only as recently as 1991 that the law stating that a husband

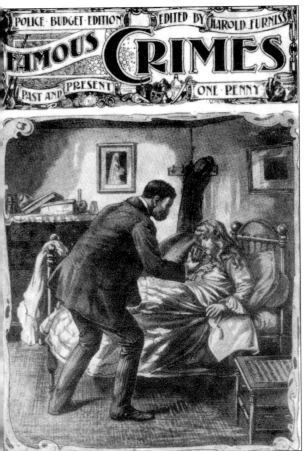

A typical scene of rape and murder from popular literature. Author's collection

could not be convicted of the rape of his wife was abolished. A wide-ranging recent study of this by Joanna Bourke has explored the lines of thought which have influenced legal process since c.1860, looking at such items as the 'No means yes' fallacy and also at related deviance such as vaginal attacks involving objects rather than the penis. Details of this are in my Bibliography.

But the basic aspects of rape in law were established in 1841 when it was stated that the hymen need not be broken in rape. In 1872, in the case of R v Mayers it was stated that saying that the victim was asleep is no defence. Then in 1850 a doctor had sex with a patient on the pretext that this was a medical treatment.

In earlier times, cases in court were rare, but when they did reach trial it was invariably a decision in favour of the plaintiff and the rapist would hang. A look at some typical cases indicates that, as usual, sexual attacks were opportunist – often taking place in fields or in a workplace when the notion that 'I could, so I did' became the ruling principle of the offence. Sexual assault involving touching, fondling and/or violence have all kinds of applications and again, in earlier times, cases were rarely heard in court.

SODOMY

In September 1806, three men were hanged at Lancaster; they were part of a group of twenty-four men who had been arrested for sodomy and related sexual offences earlier that year. Historians have made convincing arguments that, as one writer puts it, 'Moral campaigns and concern with the enforcement of the law have been identified as part of a process by which Britain's ruling elite was remade via the reformation of manners and an accompanying ethos of public and national service.' In the case of these hanged men there was a network of wealthy sodomite men involved and there was a dilemma for the magistrates: 'On the one hand, JPs were expected to adhere to ties of class and locality, while on the other, they were more significant as the instruments of central government.'

With this in mind, it is plain to see why a working-class man was often hanged for morality offences such as bestiality and sodomy, whereas other classes might go free. In fact, the crime of sodomy was no longer a capital crime in 1861.

In late Victorian England, bestiality was still severely punished. In February 1883 a certain George Miller, just seventeen, was sentenced to ten years penal servitude for bestiality with a ewe. The judge in that case admitted that he had no previous experience of hearing a case of bestiality. There was an inquiry and Miller was paroled.

OBSCENITY AND PORNOGRAPHY

This is mainly the topic of 'obscene and indecent literature' and related attitudes. The province of immorality has always been central to the church courts, but in terms of actual publications, performances and images, the main legislation is in the Licensing Acts, originating in 1662. The Obscene Publications Act of 1857 was an outcome of the fact that, back in the early eighteenth century, there had been a case before the King's Bench which made obscenity a common law offence. From 1857, magistrates had the power to act and dispose of obscene materials. There were public bodies involved also, such as the Society for the Suppression of Vice, and of course there were moral crusades, akin to those of the Temperance Movement, in the nineteenth century.

From the late Victorian period to today there have been a succession of celebrated obscenity and pornography prosecutions, but apart from these high-profile cases, there has been a large number of cases heard at the assizes of course, so ancestral misdemeanours in this area will be found at those trials.

'The suppression of vice' – a shaming punishment at Newgate. Author's collection

BIGAMY

In the Offences Against the Person Act of 1861 the offence is 'committed by any person who, while being validly married and while the marriage subsists, marries any other person during the life of the existing spouse, whether the second marriage takes place in England or elsewhere'. The defence was that with an absence of a spouse for seven years who has not been known to be living by the spouse re-marrying, then a second marriage was not bigamous. In 1889, in the case of R v Tolson, it was established that an honest belief of an invalidity of a previous marriage or the death of a spouse, a defence on that basis would be possible.

In the new world of shifting relationships and hectic emigration or travel to find work, bigamy became more common. The well-known habits of the navvy communities, having marriages 'over the brush' exemplify these changing moral practices with the decades of the Industrial Revolution at its more fierce and relentless period of change.

PROSTITUTION

'The oldest profession' has always been a touchy and difficult area of the criminal law. But as far back as 1755 there had been legislation to encourage the prosecution of people who ran 'bawdy houses'. If two ratepayers could persuade a constable to accompany them to the house in question, then there could be a prosecution. In 1847 there was an act prohibiting common prostitutes to 'assemble and continue' in pubs, and although this was developed further in the 1872 Licensing Act, it had little effect.

The mid-Victorian age was a time when many were attracted to the science of statistics, and there are figures relating to prostitution: in 1889, one writer said there were 50,000 prostitutes in London. Social commentators spent time working out how many men were likely to be infected by sexually transmitted disease in an average month in the city. But of course there were several classes of 'working girls', from the kept women of aristocrats to the women of the labouring classes making ends meet by providing for the ordinary needs of the ordinary man.

Nothing has made the general reader more aware of the scale of London prostitution than the Jack the Ripper cultural industry. Every book on this quintessential serial killer story has plenty of

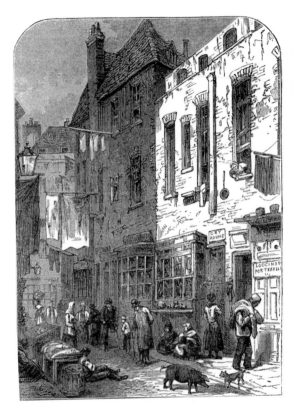

The infamous Rookery at St Giles, where prostitution thrived. Author's collection

information on the ladies of the night working Whitechapel. The cultural context of their lives is easily understood and, of course, this all relates to the Police Courts records in most cases, so the sheer scale of the sex industry at that time means that a very large number of family ancestors must have been in some way 'on the game' as a necessary part of economic survival.

ABDUCTION

The 'great age' of abduction was in the eighteenth century. The famous historian of eighteenth century Ireland, W E H Lecky, has written extensively on the London-Dublin trade in abducting wealthy young women and forcing marriage for profit. The Old Bailey sessions records are full of such cases. Of course, this was kidnapping, a common law offence. In 1714, for instance, Thomas Barnes abducted Miss Marion Harvey and was indicted for that, and also with 'unlawfully making a false affidavit for the purpose of procuring a marriage licence'.

As the Old Bailey records make clear, at a time when there was no professional police force, and certainly no detective department, it was very difficult to track down abduction cases. But as the victims were from wealthy families, there was always recourse to private agents and servants who could be detailed to protect or even pursue villains if necessary. Much depended on the networks of local legal professionals when it came to taking action against such crimes – lawyers in the city or town in question would be consulted of course. As the Old Bailey records extend to 1913, abduction cases are not too difficult to find, as of course, this was serious crime and would be dealt with also at the court of King's Bench in addition to the assizes.

In the 1861 Offences Against the Person Act, abduction was confirmed as a common law offence with the same penalty as rape – penal servitude for life as a maximum. The offence was expressed: 'Forcible abduction fo any woman with intent to marry or carnally know her.'

RESEARCH PROCESS

Rape and sexual assault

In addition to assize court records, the church courts may well have some elements of this, as sexual assaults could figure in actions for matrimonial rights. But the important aspect of this is that the King's Bench, a superior court, could hear serious cases. The King's Bench was at the top of the criminal court structure; its jurisdiction was unlimited. In theory, it could review cases and quash verdicts. With a writ called certiorari, a case could be transferred from an inferior court such as quarter sessions or manorial courts (or even assizes) but this declined after 1700 so for the modern period, assizes and church courts are still the main sources. Again, press reports are substantial from c.1800.

Sodomy

Cases of sodomy were heard at the assizes, and again, it should be remembered that the church courts would have this offence before them, usually as part of a claim for the restoration of marital rights. Such was the case of Geils v Geils in 1847 which was heard at the Arches' Court, the provincial court of Canterbury. This is presided over by the Dean of the Arches. The Geils case was at first a suit for the restitution of conjugal rights, beginning in a court of requests. It then came to the Court of Arches and in the process of that hearing it was revealed that Mr Geils had 'confessed the crime of sodomy'. Thus we have the situation in which in criminal courts there would be a life imprisonment possibility for that offence, whereas in a church court the act was sometimes a part of the whole picture presented regarding a marriage in the trial proceedings.

The Arches' Court records are at the Lambeth Palace Library and they cover the years 1554-1911. What happened was that cases came there from lower courts after an appeal. The process books of the court contain certified copies of the proceedings in the lower court submitted by the plaintiff. The criminal offences within these trials would be:

• matrimonial disputes involving criminal acts
• 'manners and morals' affair such as slander and defamation.

In the Act Books for 1554-1875 there are formal records of proceedings with supporting documents such as depositions of witnesses, sentences and stages of appeal. There are almost 10,500 cases accessible here, many on microfiche.

Again, a useful starting point for the offence is to look at the police charge books and calendars of prisoners for the relevant period.

Obscenity and Pornography
At TNA references for obscenity, sources are at the Central Criminal Court and the Supreme Court. Case papers of the Director of Public Prosecutions are gathered under the DPP series from (Misc. Series to DPP 2/5303/1) and the cases covered are mainly from the 1950s to the 1970s. The Obscene Publications Act of 1857 still applied to these cases, as it set down the fundamental guidelines on what was defined as 'obscene' and the clearest way to see the legal implications of this is to read the accounts of the infamous prosecution of D H Lawrence's publishers in 1960 for the printing in England of *Lady Chatterley's Lover*.

Bigamy
Cases of bigamy are found at the magistrates' courts and other courts. In the Old Bailey sessions records there are numerous accounts, and one insight into the range of sexual offences is to look at the

advertisements of printers, as in this from 1734, where the printer mentions a list of such crimes:

'eleven for rapes and attempts to ravish, four for sodomy, one for bigamy...' A typical case, from the same source, describes what would happen at assizes across the land in the early eighteenth century: this was the case of John Cook who was indicted for feloniously marrying Elizabeth Tooley, his former wife Ann Skelton being still alive. Martha Stanley deposed that she was at his former marriage and knew his wife to be alive. He also abused his first wife 'in a most barbarous manner' and so there was more to hear than mere bigamy. He was sentenced for 'aggravation to the crime of bigamy'. His punishment was to be branded on the hand.

Appeals for matrimonial causes are at The National Archives, at DEL and PCAP.

Prostitution

For everyday cases of crimes on the streets, the police courts, petty sessions and magistrates' courts through the centuries have these cases, briefly reported. The police records will have names and details briefly in charge books and calendars of prisoners. But there are many other sources to consult here, because the crime also involves other topics such as 'keeping of bawdy houses', brothels, procurement and of course other sources related to the lives of prostitutes, such as hospital and asylum records, church courts, prison records and records of various charitable organisations. Although the range of references is broad, the details will not be so much as to create a biographical profile in most cases. But there are Poor Law records (at MH 12).

Regarding the charitable organisations, their archives and histories may be found on their websites: the sites for NRA, A2A (Access to Archives), AIM 25 and also the Archive Hub. More details are in my Bibliography and Sources chapter.

Abduction

The Old Bailey sessions and the newspaper archives are probably the best starting-point. The cases will also be at assize records in county record office archives, and also another useful source for eighteenth-century cases is in the literature of 'Gallows speeches'. For Ireland many of these have been gathered and reprinted with commentaries by James Kelly in *Gallows Speeches* (see Bibliography). Many of these link to the holdings of university libraries and are in chapbooks and popular literature.

Most cases were reported by *The Times* and by provincial newspapers through the eighteenth and nineteenth centuries, and there are accounts in the *Annual Register* for the same period.

CASE STUDIES
Rape and sexual assault
Cases of rape and sexual assault were not often heard at the assizes at this time, 1807. Between 1814 and 1834 there were 166 such convictions in England and Wales, and of these sentences, 81 resulted in executions. Although the full circumstances are not known, it is clear that William Chapman sexually assaulted Sarah Rose on the road between Dalderby and Horncastle in August 1799. Sarah was a married woman from Roughton.

Part of the problem in unravelling rape cases lies in the blurred definitions as used throughout criminal history. Not until 1883 was the word 'rapist' first used, and that is a significant fact. As Joanna Bourke has written to explain attitudes in the early nineteenth century: 'In the words of the most prominent jurist of the 1830s, it was "almost impossible" to rape a resisting woman.'

After a deferral, Chapman was finally tried at the Lent assizes by Mr Justice Brooke and sentenced to die. He was apparently repentant in his last moments.

Sodomy
Death and persecution was usually the fate of the sodomite at this time, and historians have demonstrated that in the early years of the nineteenth century more men were either executed or imprisoned for the crime than in any other period in the history of England. Various types of bestiality are in the chronicles of crime, of course, and in Victorian England there were rare cases of sex with animals, something usually resulting in death, as in the case of an old man hanged at Ilchester for 'bestiality with a cow'.

In fact, as late as 1883 at Lincoln, there was a case of such bestiality, and it involved a young man called Miller who was given ten years penal servitude for bestiality with a ewe. But sodomy was, although equally problematical in court in some ways, more clear-cut in the early decades of the nineteenth century. In this case, the three accused had allegedly had had 'a beastly and unnatural connection with the body of Henry Hackett, a draper's apprentice'. The problem was that Hackett, only nineteen, had turned King's evidence against the three men, although he may have consented, and indeed it looks as though he did.

Reports on such things were reported in a coy and bland way, and one such account of this case was focused on the phrase, 'the commission of an unnatural crime'. Before Mr Justice Park in the September assizes, they were found guilty of the crime and of course there was scandal and revulsion, so the papers and other ephemera were full of responses to the case. Arden and Candler were from London and Candler had been a valet to the Duke of Newcastle; Doughty was a Grantham man. One contemporary broadside ballad imagines an account of the case written by the judge, and has verses such as these about Arden:

He laid his plans both deep and strong
His wickedness to hide
And thought his foul and secret ways
In safety would abide.

He was the head of all the gang.
In London did he dwell;
A fair and proper house he kept
In Pulteney Street as well...

When Lord Denman proposed changes in the criminal law in correspondence in 1837, he proposed to reduce the number of capital crimes, but kept sodomy, along with murder and treason, as hanging crimes. Between 1839 and 1848 there were 640 capital sentences in England, and these related to murder, malicious wounding, burglary, rape, robbery, arson, riot, returning from transportation, high treason and sodomy. Clearly, the offence was still rated very highly on the scale of infamy, and strangely, in the ecclesiastical courts, there were cases of marital disputes which had in them instances of sodomy as important elements in the appellants' causes of litigation.

Pornography/Obscenity
The Times reported in 1846 that 'an idler in Hungerford market' called Forder was charged with exposing indecent prints. Involved was an officer from the Society for the Suppression of Vice and he stated that 'the prisoner was offering his filthy productions to persons of both sexes in the market, and sold one of them for one penny, for which he was taken into custody.' The sentence was six weeks in prison, with hard labour.

Bigamy
In the *Liverpool Mercury* for 1869 a report from the police court told the tale of John Miller, who was on remand and charged with bigamy. A young woman named Catherine Healey had become his wife in Liverpool two years previously. She then found out about the man's first wife and reported him to the police.

The defence argued that the first wife was Miller's mother's brother's widow, and so was his aunt. That made the supposed first marriage illegal so it did not exist. Healey was therefore, Miller's proper wife. When the first wife was called to court it was shown that she was married to someone else. Miller was discharged.

More typical was the case of Robert Dalby.

Robert Dalby liked the company of women. He liked them so much that he made a habit of marrying them. The fact that the English legal system dictated that one wife at a time is permissible, and not having several at one time, did not deter him. Dalby was fifty-six when he was finally tracked down and he stood in court in Bradford in this precariously illegal situation. He had four 'wives' at that time.

This might all seem little more than a sad and farcical situation, but Dalby was also in the habit of using his fists against women. At the time of his arrest he was living in Cleckheaton and was sharing his home with Mary Copley, but he had three others, and the last of these was with Mary Ann Mortimer. It is in his life with this particular Mary that we learn about his nasty side. Dalby, only two months before his appearance in court for bigamy, had been charged with a violent assault on his first Mary.

The man had been two months in prison, and when he walked out again a free man, the officers were waiting for him with the more serious charge ready. After zealous enquiries around the area, it emerged that Dalby had married six times. Behind him lay a trail of emotional chaos; one of the women had died, and another had disappeared without trace. He was a man of mystery who had made a terrible mess of many who had the misfortune to meet him and to fall for his considerable charm.

He was ostensibly a schoolmaster by profession, so we have to assume that he found some time to earn a living, in between the time required for courting and setting up home with this succession of ladies. Police did ascertain the right documentary information about his current marriage when arrested: he had indeed married Mary Coley at Calverley in 1845. It must have taken a very long time to track down the other three who make up the total messy picture of the man's life, but they were all found and informed of the truth.

More recently, he had ventured into Lancashire where he would not be so well known, and presumably where he was less likely to run into former wives or even relatives of those wives. He married Mary Ann Roberts in Hulme, near Manchester, at Holy Trinity Church; he also wed Margaret Scholes at the parish church in Rochdale in 1865. Finally, within the last year before his arrest, and just months before settling down with his Mary at Cleckheaton, he had stood at the altar to become the husband of the Mary Copley he had taken to beating, and this was in Birstall, in August 1870. This is very difficult to absorb, but it covers most of the marriages.

Amazingly, Robert Dalby had lived for a while with all of these, and had children with them. There were Dalby children across the Pennines, and also scattered in Wales as well: this was to one Ann Roberts, and the pluralist, speaking in court to an awestruck array of listeners, referred to the Welsh wedding as 'the only honourable marriage of the lot'. In fact, when pressed to explain his behaviour with some semblance of meaning and sense, if that were possible, all he could say was that he had been spending years of his life doing little more than 'seeking an honourable woman to settle down with'.

The dark shadow beneath this ridiculous lifestyle was that of the pleasure he clearly took in striking and beating his women. Not only was there a trail of illegal alliances behind him, but also a number of young women who had felt the back of his hand. Another spell behind bars was waiting for him – this time for a considerably longer period. It is on record that all his former wives were tracked down and interviewed, and we can only imagine the stunned and alarmed reactions of so many women being told, in effect, that their children were bastards and their marriage certificates were invalid. They had all wondered where the husband had gone, why the money had stopped arriving, and who was going to feed and clothe the families.

There is no doubt that the rogue philanderer, Robert Dalby, spent no time worrying about these questions in his cell.

Prostitution

This first case shows that coroners' inquests are a worthwhile source for this offence. This one was held at the Red Lion in Middlesex, Westbourne Green in November 1826. It relates the sad suicide of a prostitute, and illustrates that the historian learns the biography of the subject more thoroughly when there is a personal tragedy. Ann Owen's body was recovered from the Paddington Canal and the story emerged that she was 'lately come out of Kent in great distress'. She

The Justice Room at the Mansion House. Author's collection

had been refused assistance by her friends and that 'poverty and the wretchedness of her situation had driven her to prostitution'. The verdict did not use the word suicide.

In contrast, the Westminster sessions, in November 1827 discussed the case of Phoebe Isaacs who kept a 'house of ill fame' in White Hart Yard. She had been arrested with three of her girls when they were in the act of 'holding a gentleman by the arm'. The report gives a clear picture of the forces of law:

'The evidence of Nott, a beadle, Ryan, a watchman and Bond, a conductor of a patrol proved that she nightly promenaded the streets in the vicinity of the theatres, for the purpose of prostitution.' Isaacs was sentenced to one month at Tothill Fields prison.

Abduction

In the time when the Old Bailey was the centre of attraction for everyone on both sides of the law, there were tradesmen about who were only too happy to cash in on the sensational and sad lives of villains – especially those whose lives had ended dangling on a rope at Tyburn. One such retailer was Richard Wam of the Bible and Sun at Warwick Lane, Amen Corner, London. Among his sick and bizarre items for sale there was a series of chapbooks with narratives on them, and one of these published in 1730 was this, as advertised:

> The case of Mr. Dan. Kimberley, attorney at law, executed at Dublin, May 27, 1730, for assisting Bradock Mead to marry Bridget Rending, an heiress. Contained in his declaration and dying words, delivered to the Rev. Mr. Derry, at the place of execution, and recommended to Dean Percival, John Hacket, Esq, and two other gentlemen, to see it published. Price: three pence.

Behind that smart piece of advertising there lies not only the complex tale of a learned and educated man who fell into deep trouble, but also a story typical of its age and place – one more abduction in hundreds, a trade (and a crime) totally heartless and unscrupulous – and of course, a capital offence. Kimberley's last dying speech tract was headed, 'Daniel Kimberley, Gentleman'.

Those words were unusual for a gallows tale, and his date with death was an meticulously recorded as the vents of his own story: 'Executed at St Stephen's Green on Wednesday, May 27th, 1730 at 38 minutes past three o'clock in the afternoon.'

The famous historian of eighteenth century Ireland, W E H Lecky, in his account of the spate of abductions of heiresses in that time, explains how many people ascribed them to sectarian enmity, yet he finds little evidence of that. But there were certainly many varieties of abduction, and whatever their nature, they were brutal and cruel. At its worst, an abduction could be like this one, as described by Lecky:

> On a Sunday in the June of 1756, the Rev. John Armstrong was celebrating divine service in the Protestant church in the town of Tipperary, Susannah Grove being among the congregation. In the midst of the service Henry Grady, accompanied by a body of men armed with blunderbusses, pistols, and other weapons, called out to the congregation that anyone who stirred would be shot, struck the clergyman on the arm with a hanger and... hastening to the pew where Susannah was sitting, dragged her out...

But we are not dealing with this variety in Kimberley's story, and, as Lecky points out, the Kimberley case is unusual because he was a Protestant, pointing out that 'Among the few persons who were executed for abduction in Ireland was an attorney named Kimberley, at a time when no-one but a professing Protestant could be enrolled in that profession.'

Here then, we have a case of a lawyer and a Protestant being hanged for an offence for which few were hanged. What was so heinous about this particular abduction? Or did Kimberley have powerful enemies?

His own account of the events of the abduction of Bridget Reading (not Rending, as the London printer had it) is expectedly, full of bad luck stories and of his being an innocent dupe. Making sense of Kimberley's own garbled and complicated account of what happened, there emerges a bare outline of a plausible story: he was a lawyer and so would have appeared to be hardly a 'heavy' when it came to applying some pressure on the intended abduction and forced marriage of your Bridget Reading, for that is what lies at the heart of this story. Kimberley was contacted by an unscrupulous adventurer called Braddock Mead, with an assignment of visiting the nurse who had the guardianship of Bridget. Now, Kimberley argued that the old couple who had Bridget in care were also after her inheritance, and he said that he was told 'there was a considerable sum of money due to her... she never having received a penny from her father, who was an ill man'.

The lawyer then found out that Mead, back in London, had more knowledge of Bridget's situation than he had at first said because he took out articles with a man called Dodamy with a plan to sell Bridget's estate for the then huge sum of £3,600. The pressure was then on Kimberley to get a desired result in his negotiations to prise Bridget from her guardian and to speed her to the altar with Mead. Again and again, Kimberley insisted that there had been no forced marriage: 'soon after, and by my consent, and inducement, Mead applied to said Bridget by way of courtship and on 11th April, 1728, said Mead married her in Dublin, when and where no force, threats, or compulsion was made use of by any person towards said Bridget to come into said marriage.'

Understanding this case is all a matter of believing Kimberley was 'sold out' to the law or not. His argument was that Mead was largely responsible for duping him and setting him up, as he was seen as the actual agent of the affair, and so would be assumed to have used force on the girl. When Mead was arrested and imprisoned and the network was about to be destroyed (and heads to roll) Mead was threatened by Mr Reading to apply a charge of rape against him unless he had the marriage annulled, Kimberley was apparently 'stooged'. He did understand that the right moves had been attempted, though. Applications were made to the Doctors' Commons, and though the intentions may have been good, to dissolve the contract, perhaps the Doctors' Commons was not the right place to go. Later, Dickens was to call that institution of Doctors of Law 'a cosy, dozy, old-fashioned and time-forgotten, sleepy-headed little family party'.

As with all such convoluted narratives of crime, it all depends who is believed at the time, and by the people who matter. Daniel Kimberley was clearly not believed; we have his side of the story, but we also have the weight of history and statistics to show how hard the authorities were coming down on abductions of heiresses. It may be that, in the end, Kimberley was being harshly punished as a precedent to other professional gentleman not be involved in that nefarious and amoral trade.

He faced his death on the scaffold with courage, offering to dramatic entertainment to the crowd. He even ended his speech with the surprising attitude of forgiveness: 'As for my prosecutors, or such as have persecuted me. Or fought any perjurious or indirect ways to take away my life, I freely forgive them.' Reading between the lines, there is still rancour there, and a 'spin' towards showing himself in a better light than his enemies. But, as with many others in his final minutes, his main concern was for his reputation: 'In order to prevent the publishing of any false or spurious accounts of me... I do therefore humbly entreat my very worthy friends, the Rev. Dean Percival, Mr Derry, John Hacket, Edmund Fenner... to order the printing and publishing of this declaration.'

He did have some friends (Dean Percival has gone down in history as one of the men who lampooned Jonathan Swift in a satirical poem) but clearly their exertions were not strenuous enough to save him from the gallows.

Chapter 8

TREASON AND POLITICAL CRIMES

TREASON

The Treason Act of 1351 defines the various categories of high treason, as opposed to petty treason (discussed in Chapter 1 as a version of punishment for murder). These are most importantly: (a) 'compassing or imagining the death of the King, of his Queen, or of their eldest son and heir; (b) violating the King's consort or the King's eldest daughter unmarried, or the wife of the eldest son and heir; (c) levying war against the King in his realm; (4) adhering to the King's enemies in his realm, giving them aid or comfort in the realm or elsewhere. Following this, the Treason Act of 1795 specified 'compassing the death, or any harm tending to the death, wounding, imprisonment or restraint of the King'.

Of course, treason offences are always very high profile, so there is no problem in finding information. The really famous cases, such as that of Sir Walter Raleigh, Sir Roger Casement and William Joyce, provide all the essential elements of the law in this respect. Lord Denning, in Landmarks in the Law (1984) has assessed these in terms of the 1351 statute, and he focuses in each case on a fundamental legal question such as, in the case of Joyce (Lord Haw Haw): 'The trial of William Joyce took place in 1945 after the end of the Second World War. It raised another new point. He was an American citizen. As such he owed no allegiance to the King. But he held a British passport. Could he be convicted of High Treason?' The answer was yes. He was hanged.

SEDITION

Sedition refers to acts done with an intention of exciting disaffection or contempt against the Sovereign or constitution of England. It also includes any attempt to excite 'feelings of ill-will and hostility between different classes of society', or 'exciting persons to crime or the

A poster giving an account of an attempt at assassination. Author's collection

disturbance of the peace'. Your ancestor may well have been involved in such offences in the late eighteenth century, or in the Regency period in particular, when war with France and the impact on Britain of the French Revolution created a profound fear and paranoia in the riling and propertied classes. If ancestors were political radicals such as Chartists then the search will be across a wide variety of sources. If they were printers or writers, they could easily have been prosecuted in that touchy and sensitive time for the social hierarchies of the land.

An insight into the nature of sedition in the Regency period is seen in the declaration of the Hull magistrates in 1817, a time of widespread privation and radicalism. They wrote to *The Times*: 'At the same time that we most feelingly sympathize with various classes of society in their sufferings, we are anxious to testify our decided disapprobation of those who are endeavouring to excite discontent.' They were responding to a statement by the Prince Regent and the Houses of Parliament on the subject of the perceived 'alienations and disaffections of the people' to the government. Nine magistrates and the Recorder of Hull, Robert Osborne, signed the statement.

ESPIONAGE
The first Official Secrets Act of 1911 and others, in 1920, 1939 and 1989 were concerned with breaches of official confidence. In times of war in particular, there were cases of espionage before the superior courts and consequently in the courts of appeal, so if an ancestor breached one of those Acts, it was a serious affair and the documentation will be voluminous.

POLITICAL CRIME
It has to be noted here that in the court records and press reports on all of the above, there will be blurred lines of demarcation; for instance sedition and mutiny might run together at times, and the Chartist demonstrations are a useful case in point. In the 1830s in particular, there were large-scale demonstrations of Chartists across the country. In Leeds, the so-called 'Physical Force' Chartists (as opposed to the 'Moral Force' thinkers) drilled with arms on Woodhouse Moor. Obviously, there was a danger of their behaviour becoming treasonous; their publications could be seditious and some activities would break the Riot Act. If Chartists gathered for meetings, that could breach the Combination Acts. Therefore if your ancestor was any kind of political radical, the charges in respect of specific actions might be across a range of offences.

RESEARCH PROCESS
Treason
Treason trials were in a superior court: the King's Bench (Crown side – dealing with criminal cases); the High Court of Justice or the Courts of Appeal (criminal and military); in Northern Ireland and Scotland the Supreme Courts, and at times the Judicial Committee of the House of Commons. In the Court of King's Bench the years covered are from 1675 to 1875. The King's Bench, Crown Side, is the highest court of criminal law. At TNA the search for named defendants begins with

draft rule books and depositions at KB21 and KB 36. Then there are related indexes at IND 1/6669-6677 for London and Middlesex. The provincial defendants are at IND 1/6680-6684. Sentences and depositions are at KB1. Indictment files are at KB10.

For treason, however, there is such a great deal of material in printed secondary sources that these are easily available in a good law library. An internet search will quickly bring a list of treason trials and then the researcher can follow up with dates and names.

Sedition

Your ancestor's case in this respect would have been heard in one of the higher courts, but of course they would stand in the circuit assizes first. Newspapers have always given prominence to this, and periodicals of a left-wing persuasion will be other good sources.

At TNA look at miscellaneous papers of the Treasury Solicitor at TS 24/7/80, TS 24/7/72 and all the 24/7 series. Also useful are the Public Order Committee report CAB 24/179, the Report by the Committee on Fascism CAB 129/8, the Foreign Office correspondence of the political department for 1966 and the 1921 Monthly Review of Revolutionary Movements.

Espionage

After the Official Secrets Act of 1911 and the following acts, there has been a massive accumulation of documents regarding spycatching activities on the Home Front in both world wars. TNA have a great deal of information on this and have published a book with details of all important sources: British Intelligence: Secrets, Spies and Sources by Stephen Twigge, Edward Hampshire and Graham Macklin. This covers information on all important related documents at TNA, including topics such as domestic intelligence, military and naval intelligence and the Special Operations Executive. The main sources for the Great War are in 'Spotlight on History' at TNA which looks at the First World War, and the PF series KV 2 /822. There is also a feature on the execution of German spies. For World War Two, the handbook is the best starting point as there is a massive amount of information.

Political Crime

The annals of Chartism are at the centre of this, and there is a free website, www.chartists.net run by Mark Crail. This covers the years

1839 to 1848 when the great Chartist petitions were circulated and presented to government. There is also a Chartist periodical press to explore, accessible online through the British Nineteenth Century Newspapers facility from the British Library. Regional press gave full accounts of Chartist meetings and protest.

Many Chartists were destined for prisons and houses of correction and the issue then was their status as prisoners: if they were political prisoners, did they have to work the treadmill, do normal prison work and so on? The prison records will show these names, as will census records of course.

Military records and court proceedings will include this offence also, and if dates are known, then press reports are the best starting point. One of the most useful aspects of this topic is that there will be extra information in some of the massive sources online, such as The Black Sheep Index (see my Bibliography and Resource guide).

At TNA the feature, 'Chartism – Your Archives' has a lot of information for 1836-1852 under the BT 41 series and the Prison Commission at HO 10/31, HO 100 and HO 102. Old Bailey sessions papers also have Chartist cases for 1836-1852.

CASE STUDIES

Treason for espionage provides full documentation, for almost every conflict. But in world wars we have biographies and very detailed trial notes. Also, the judges and appeal courts have more information. The publications of Sir Travers Humphreys and Lord Denning for instance (see Bibliography) gives accounts of spy trials. This case study section comes from a mix of these sources, and shows the need never to overlook smaller provincial archives, because the main source is from Doncaster Archives at Balby.

Before Steve Wade, the hangman, began his main work in Yorkshire, he had a job with Albert Pierrepoint hanging another spy that turned out to be a terrible ordeal. Wade took a few notes on jobs, and a typical one is this one on William Cooper at Bedford in 1940. Tom and Albert were the official hangmen, but Wade must have been there to observe and to learn, because he made these notes:

William Henry Cooper at Bedford, aged 24. Height, five feet five and A half inches. Weight 136lbs. Drop 8feet one inch. Assisted to Scaffold. Hanged 9 a.m. on Nov. 26 1940.

He notes that the personnel present were 'Pierrepoint, Wade and Allen' but that does not tally with the official record.

As time went on he wrote more, as in the case of Mancini: 'Three appeals with the House of Lords.' But the ordeal was to come with the execution of the spy Karel Richter. Richter's records have now been released and we know that his mission was to deliver funds and a spare wireless crystal to another spy. He was given a code and money and also a supply of secret ink and was even briefed on what to say if interrogated. Acccording to some opinions, his arrival on espionage work was part of a 'double-cross' system which meant that agents were captured and given an option either to work as double agents or to face the gallows.

Richter was parachuted into Hertfordshire in 1941 and it appears that Churchill wanted him executed, as other agents had landed and not been hanged. That might be arguable, but what happened, according to MI5, is that Richter landed on the 14 May and that war reserve constable Boot at London Colney saw a lorry driver talking to a man who turned out to be the spy. Sergeant Palmer of St Albans was informed and came to assist. Richter was taken to Fleetville Police Station and there he showed a Czech passport. When searched, he had a ration book, a compass, cash and a map of East Anglia.

Richter was seen by a girl, Florrie Cowley (nee Chapman) who recalls going to visit her divisional campsite, of the guides, at Colney heath and that she and a friend went into a storage hut. There they saw evidence of very recent occupation. She wrote in a memoir,

'We quickly came out to think the situation over. Being wartime there were no vagabonds, tramps etc. around so who could be living there? We then thought a German spy could have dropped...' They were right. Photographs survive of Richter going back to the field with army and police to find his buried equipment. Richter stands in one photograph, pointing, while surrounded by personnel. He was destined to be Pierrepoint and Wade's client on 10 December 1941.

Wade kept notes on what happened that day. It was a horrendous experience for the young hangman, so early in his career. First he wrote, 'Karl Richter, 29 five feet and eleven and a half inches. 172 lbs. Execution: good under the circumstances.' That has to be one of the greatest understatements ever written. Richter was athletic, strong and determined to cause the maximum resistance when the hangmen arrived at the death-cell. Wade wrote:

> On entering cell to take prisoner over and pinion him he made a
> bolt towards the door. I warded him off and he then charged the
> wall at a terrific force with his head. This made him most violent.
> We seized him and strapped his arms at rear... The belt was
> faulty, not enough eyelid holes, and he broke away from them. I
> shouted to Albert 'He is loose' and he was held by warders until
> we made him secure. He could not take it and charged again for
> the wall screaming HELP ME.

Things were still very difficult, as the man then had to be
manhandled by several warders. Even at the scaffold, Richter fought:

> ... he then tried to get to the opposite wall over trap. Legs splayed.
> I drew them together and see Albert going to the lever. I shout
> wait, strap on legs and down he goes. As rope was fixed around
> his neck he shook his head and the safety ring, too big, slips...

Wade's notes have a tone of relief as he writes finally, 'Neck broken
immediately.'

At the end of his notes he wrote that he said something to Albert, a
comment along the lines of 'I would not miss this for fifty pounds...'

Richter actually stated under questioning that he had declined to
take a part in the 'double cross system'. He had been a marine engineer
and had a child in the USA. He was interned and returned to Germany
after trying to return to America. In Germany he was recruited by the
Abwehr (the German intelligence and counter intelligence organisation).
Nigel West, in his history of MI5, has a coda to add to Steve Wade's
terrible memoir:

> The grisly scene had a profound effect on all those present, and,
> indirectly, on some other Abwehr agents. Several months later
> Pierrepoint and his chief assistant, Steve Wade, carried out an
> execution at Mountjoy in Dublin. News of Richter's final
> moments reached Gunther Schutz and his fellow internees... Irish
> warders gleefully recounted the details of the struggle on the
> scaffold, sending Richter's former colleagues into a deep
> depression.

Sedition

In 1817, the Bow Street constables arrested a man suspected of 'being concerned in seditious practices'. He was acquitted, but this shows how vigilant the law was at that time of national crisis. In the same week, a schoolmaster in Glasgow was arrested and charged with sedition. He had written and printed some pamphlets that were critical of the government, and another teacher, from Carmunnock, was gaoled for 'treasonable practices'. Many offenders took to the road for this, after rewards were announced for their apprehension. A typical example if that of one J McEwen who was a carding master in the Gorbals in 1817. He was accused of treasonable practices and of administering unlawful oaths – the latter a capital offence.

If the place of the ancestor's trial is known, the press reports are a good first call in the quest.

Political Crime

In 1840, W J Williams produced a report on prisoners in York Castle who had taken part in the Bradford Chartist rising. One man, Emanuel Hutton, twenty-eight, had been sentenced to eighteen months hard labour in Wakefield gaol. He was a woolcomber, his condition described as 'much distressed'. Williams reported that Hutton was aware that there had been a movement known as the 'Physical Force' Chartists, and it seems that he read the radical newspapers and had been on the margin of events.

The prisoner told how he had joined a crowd, not really knowing what was happening, and was led into trouble: 'I saw a man who told me to follow him… I saw a lot of men who bade me go into the market place with them – one gave me the gun.' The hard fact is that in the year building up to the risings in South Wales and then in Lancashire and Yorkshire at this time, many of the plans conceived had involved a desire to murder police officers. On Woodhouse Moor in nearby Leeds, Feargus O'Connor, leader of the 'Physical Force' men, had been drilling his forces. It was a national emergency, all based on the widespread political exclusion of the working men. O'Connor had been a well-known figure in this context around Yorkshire for some time, having done his first northern lecture tour in 1835. He had then published his newspaper, the *Northern Star*, in Leeds from July 1837.

The Chartists wanted reform of the suffrage; the 1832 Reform Act had excluded those who were working with their hands in the toughest occupations that were making the Industrial Revolution possible; the Bradford woolcombers were a significant part of that deprivation, and they were fertile ground for the demagogues, and indeed for those who thought violence was the best way to achieve results.

The preparations for a full-scale confrontation with the forces of law had been on a terrifying level of agitation and fear, as the authorities saw it. In 1839, the wide space of Hartshead Moor, or Peep Green as it then was, was the scene of one of the largest Chartist rallies of the time. The area was like a fair, with over a hundred huts put up for the sale of food and drink. Some said that half a million people had turned up, but a more realistic figure was perhaps 200,000. This was on 18 October, and O'Connor was there, talking about the death of tyrants; another leader, Bussey, insisted that the best thing Bradford men could do was buy guns. Hartshead had been in use before, back in May 1837, when it staged a Poor Law meeting. It was fast becoming a spot in Bradford with a disturbing reputation for the local agencies of law.

Men did listen to Bussey, and they went to arm themselves. Justices of the Peace started taking depositions from shopkeepers who had had visits from desperate men out to use rifles; William Egan, a Bradford gunsmith, recalled how he had had visits from such locals. He stated, later when he was a witness: '… a person whom I did not know and who appeared to be in the capacity of a labourer called at my shop and asked me if I had any guns or bayonets by me, to which I answered that I had not.' Pressure was being exerted; men were desperate to arm and to take on the local authority. Egan said that in one period of about ten days, he 'had been applied to in order to alter muskets which have been brought to me without the stocks….'

Something nasty was brewing, and the law employed spies – *agents provocateurs* – to infiltrate the radical activists. It was beginning to look as though Bradford would be the centre of a massive revolt of the excluded and oppressed people. James Harrison was an informer of this kind. In December 1839, he gave an account of what was going on with the extremists. He had been to a meeting at the Queen's Head, four miles from the city centre, and there he heard that there were around 260 men armed and ready. There was also a London Chartist at this meeting, and Harrison must have been worried. He recalled: 'In the bar there was this delegate, George Flinn, two men from the Queen's Head and myself. The man from London looked earnestly at me and asked Flinn if he knew me. Flinn said he had known me for three years and I was as good as any man in the room…'

The magistrates were frightened, and wrote to the Home Secretary, expressing their concerns. These were E C Lister of Manningham, Matthew Thompson, H W Hird and W R Stansfield. They wrote about 'violent harangues of evil disposed and Revolutionary speakers' and they felt that 'some violent outrage' was about to take place.

What did actually happen in 1840? The leader of the abortive revolt was Robert Peddie, and his narrative explains most things that took place. The plans of Peddie and his peers must have been terrifying to the place: Bradford then had a population of 66,000 and a police force of half a dozen men. There was no real police force outside London, and these events took place only ten years after Peel's first Police Act. It is no wonder that localities relied on the army in these situations, so naturally a bunch of ordinary labouring men would have no chance of success, and this was the case with Peddie's plans. James Harrison outlined Peddie's notions of a co-ordinated revolt, involving miners as well as the Bradford people. Harrison met with a group of insurgents at the Junction tavern on Leeds new Road, and the plan was to go to Leeds and set fire to the magazine. Peddie's talk certainly included the desire to achieve the Chartists' aims – universal suffrage, no qualification for voting rights and so on. But there was another agenda, feeding other, nefarious discontents as well.

Everything was nipped in the bud; plans and leaders were known. Major General Charles Napier was given command of what was called the Northern District, in 1839. He soon had men billeted around the West Riding conurbation – for instance forty-two men in Halifax in forty-two houses; altogether in Yorkshire he had a thousand troops. He had to act quickly; very extreme things were happening, such as a book in circulation in Halifax about facing barricades and how to face cavalry with a pike.

Peddie was given three years' imprisonment after the Chartist Trials of March 1840. O'Connor had stolen the limelight, and his trial was extremely protracted. In the end, no policemen were killed in the streets, but that was soon to come, just eight years later. D G Wright has noted that Peddie's colourful radical career made him enemies on his own side of the law, too. Wright says that at one point 'the Scots Chartists decided they had had enough of this wilful, self-centred and histrionic man…'

Chapter 9

DESTINATIONS:
PRISON, ASYLUM, HULKS, TRANSPORTATION

PRISON HISTORY AND RECORDS

The history of prisons in Britain in forms other than in castles and other holding locations begins in the sixteenth century with the London Bridewell. Although there were earlier gaols, such as the one at Hexham, run by the Archbishop of York's bailiff as early as the fourteenth century, for the purposes of consistent records, the houses of correction are the first organised nationwide gaols. They were also know as 'bridewells' after the first one, as that became a generic term. In 1609, justices in each county had to establish a house of correction.

The houses of correction were local, controlled by the local justices of the peace and panels of other dignitaries; they were mainly for a mix of debtors and remand prisoners. Convicted prisoners would be housed also, but as many of these as possible were transported, hanged or, later, sent to the hulks ostensibly to await transportation. The records of these early gaols are quite substantial, and there were eighteenth and nineteenth century reports written on them firstly by John Howard, whose book, *The State of the Prisons* was published in 1777 and then by others, notably by the *Gentleman's Magazine* in the first years of the nineteenth century.

As the houses of correction were criticised by the 1830s, and as other models for experimental prisons were put forward, the large penitentiaries were built, the first being Millbank, opened in 1816 on the site of what is today the Tate Gallery. By 1877 the prisons were nationalised and in 1878 thirty-eight prisons were closed, so that is an important date for family historians to bear in mind. There were seventy-five local prisons left after that date.

In the early twentieth century the Borstals were started. As the

'The History of Newgate' a popular publication c.1880. Author's collection

twentieth century advanced, so the number and categories of prisons developed and changes were constantly in progress, so prison records need close attention. The prison records within the establishments were substantial; surgeons kept journals, as did governors, and there were plenty of official reports produced. The copious materials in the papers of the House of Commons provide excellent information on all aspects of prison life in the nineteenth century, including plans of prison design and questionnaires given to staff.

TNA provides a detailed and well organised guide to searching prison records, and the list of documents which should be consulted first in the search are in the series ADM, AO and B 1-8, followed by Old Bailey depositions; judges' reports (at HO6, 12, 13 and 14). Criminal petitions are at HO17-19 for 1815 – 1854.

This is a summarised list of holdings at TNA:

ADM 101 1785-1963 medical journals.

AO3 1539-1886 accounts – various.

B2 1662-1869 Court of Bankruptcy and gaolers' returns.

B3 1759-1911 Bankruptcy Commission Files.

B4 1710-1849 Bankruptcy Commission Docket Books.

B6 1733-1925 Bankruptcy registers.

B8 1820-1870 Bankruptcy indexes (relating to B6 and B5).

CRIM. 1 -12 Old Bailey records covering 1833-1971.

E 389 Exchequer, miscellaneous. This has valuable records for earlier periods, including gaolers' bills, payments for hanging, outlawry rolls and lists of prisoners sent to hulks.

HO6 Home Office judges' returns for 1816-1840.

HO12-14 for 1849-1871 the Criminal Entry Books, registers of papers and warrant books of the Home Office Criminal Department. The Home Office was established in 1782 and a massive amount of materials from the provincial gaols went to their Criminal Department. Here will be found such things as pardons, pleas for Respites (pardons by the Home Secretary and the Recorder of London's panel).

HO15-19 Committals to the old Bailey, warrant books, criminal; petitions and outcomes of petitions.

HO20 Prison correspondence and papers. This relates to convict ships.

HO23 Registers of county prisons for 1847-1866. This is a really useful first step, listing registers of prisoners in ten county prisons, giving lots of material on the basic biographies of prisoners.

HO24 Prison registers and returns for 1838-1875.

HO26-27 The criminal registers for Middlesex and England and Wales. These show all persons registers as having an indictable offence – series 1 in Middlesex for 1791-1849, and series 2 for all counties from 1805-1892.

HO 40-46 provides a mass of material, including, at HO 40 material on Luddites, Chartist and other political prisoners.

HO45 is the main Home Office collection for 1839-1979 and covers many subjects, including: courts, convicts, treason, sedition and transportation.

HO47 for 1784-1829 covers a vast number of judges' reports. In the catalogue, it is possible to have a summary of the person and offence/trial online.

HO77 The Newgate Calendar 1782-1853.

HO140 the Calendars of prisoners for 1868-1971 This has trial lists of trials at assizes and quarter sessions, done alphabetically by county.

HO144 This is another place to check if the ancestor in question was a 'political' such as a Fenian: it covers disturbances and explosives, for instance.

HO247 Borstal Association Reports – registers and Files from 1905-1977. Here, there are personal profiles of boys in Borstals, with photographs. Many of these stories lead into army records, as a large number of subjects joined the army in the Great War.

HO336 has prison records from the Prison Commission and Home Office Prison Department. These were files formerly kept in the prisons, and refer to capital offences.

STATE TRIALS

For treason, the reference is KB8 for the Court of King's Bench, Crown Side. These are of famous state trials such as Anne Boleyn, Guy Fawkes etc.

PRISON RECORDS – PRISON COMMISSION

For 1770-1951 the Series 1 registers and indexes of prisoners and habitual criminals provides a wealth of prison material, from order books to quarter sessions calendars.

PCOM 3 and 4 provide details of licences from 1853-1887 and are searchable online.

PCOM 6-9 provides registers, indexes, registered papers and papers on individual prisoners.

PRIS 1-3 cover the Fleet prison and so these provide an excellent source for research on debtors in London.

PRIS 4 covers the King's Bench from 1719-1862 and again has details of debtors, including the Marshalsea, from 1843 when three prisons were amalgamated.

PRIS 5-10 has King's/Queen's Bench prisons records from 1780-1862.

SEDITION

For this, see TS24 on Miscellaneous papers on sedition cases for 1732-1901. This has printed pamphlets, literature and journalism related to sedition in the period, notably in the Regency and in the 1900-01 Boer War seditious literature.

ASYLUMS AND CARE OF THE INSANE

Within the prison records, there are these useful sources for convicts in care:

MH51, for 1798-197, the Lunacy Commission and Board of Control – correspondence and papers. This has law officers' opinions from

One of the many destinations of the insane – the new Caledonian Asylum.
Author's collection

1857, and orders for the removal of lunatics from asylums; also with returns form gaols for 1858 concerning insane prisoners.

HO343 has Home Office Mental Patients Files for 1927-1986. The Home Office Secretary is responsible for offenders ordered from courts to special hospitals. Also see MH103 for equivalent files from the hospitals.

For a full picture of the social history of asylums see my Bibliography, especially the study by Marlene A Arieno.

THE HULKS

From 1775 criminals who would normally have been sent to America had to be held at home. Ships were then used as prisons; known as 'hulks', these were supposed to be temporary measures, but in fact they existed for decades, and a report in 1847 noted that these were awful places, with intolerable neglect evident everywhere. Between 1776 and 1795 one third of the total number of 5,722 prisoners died in the hulks. By 1830 there were ten hulks, holding 4,400 prisoners.

We can have a glimpse of a convict of 1791, found guilty of stealing plate and clothes in Lincoln. He was initially sentenced to death but this was commuted to fourteen years of transportation, but in fact he

The Discovery convict ship lying at Deptford, 1829. Author's collection

spent two years on board the Cares hulk. His case is summarised in a judge's report (HO47/13/163).

Details of prison hulks and their records are at the TNA, covering the years 1802-1834 at HO9/I to 9/15 and these are given by the name of each hulk ship, from the *Bellerophon* to the *York*, with separate dates for each ship.

TRANSPORTATION

The first transportation was to America and the West Indies; then in 1787 transportation to Australia began, and was to last for eighty years until 1867. The idea of transporting convicts meant that there was a serious punishment that was an alternative to hanging. After 1718 transportation to America meant that the convicts with conditional pardons would have a fourteen-year sentence there. For non-capital offences the stretch was seven years. The 1853 Penal Servitude Act began to step down the flow of transported convicts by stating that convicts would be housed in gaols at home, and Section 9 of that act initiated the early licence system know as 'ticket of leave'. It is an interesting contextual point that criminal records in the ten

A typical hulk prison ship: thirty-four prisoners waiting for transportation.
Author's collection

years after that act will show frequent references to supposed crime waves done by 'ticket of leave men' such as the widespread garrotting panic of 1862-3. Police records and court records, as well as press reports in these years will show that trend.

TNA have two research guides on their website with full information on this. At the heart of research for his is Peter Wilson Coldham's book, *The Complete Book of Emigrants in Bondage 1614-1775*. This has an alphabetical list of all convicts of the period. From there, the sequence of investigations is:

1) Look at assize records for a felony, a serious crime, as transportation up to 1718 was the alternative to death. After that date, and for lesser offences and terms of seven years, see assizes or the Old Bailey sessions.

2) For later convicts – from the period 1787-1857 – again, start with assize records and press reports for the cases in question. Then:

3) Check in the standard printed books, Criminal Ancestors or Bound for Australia (see Bibliography) because all the documents available are listed and reproduced there.

4) Look at the transportation registers at HO26 (Middlesex) or HO27 Middlesex prisoners not tried at the Old Bailey and HO11 for 1787-1871 transportation registers.

5) Check the Home Office petitions for clemency at HO17 (for 1819-1839) and HO18 (for 1839-1854). Petitions for clemency are at HO17-19.

Everything depends on the location of the trajectory of the criminal's destiny in court. The following steps should help:

Find out where the trial was held - assize courts within the circuit relevant to where the offence was committed. Dates and places of trial are usually in the prison registers for hulks – as above, in HO9. All the above convict hulks references apply here. But checking on assize records is done by looking at TNA Assizes: Criminal Trials 1559-1971. In sheriffs' assize vouchers there may be more related material because these materials have information on the assize hearings also. Of course, the Old Bailey sessions are relevant here, and it has also to be recalled that the palatinate courts were separate from the main system up to 1830, so their records might be relevant to your search. The palatinate of Chester has material in TNA at CHES20, 21 and 25. For Wales, these equivalent records are at the National Library of Wales, Aberystwyth (see Bibliography). For the other palatinates, see DURH15 and 19 and PL25-28.

What the convicts would have looked like in Australia.
The author

For the records relating to transportation itself, petitions are at HO17 and 18, 48, 49, 54 and 56. The judges' reports at HO47 give information on commutations and pardons. At the centre of all this are the convict transportation registers at HO11 because these give details of the vessels, term of sentence, agents and place of conviction. Medical reports on convicts in transit are at ADM 101 for 1817-53.

In Australia, there were Colonial Office Records and for this one needs to check the Colonial Office Index. But in HO10 there is a census list with convicts named, and some are more complete than others. Also in HO10 are details of ticket of leave arrangements and pardons. Transcripts of census returns are also in Australia: see The Library of Australian History, 17 Mitchell Street, North Sydney 2060 Sydney, Australia. TNA also has a list of useful publications with muster rolls for various penal colonies and convict ships.

Finally, special mention must be made of David T Hawkings' *Criminal Ancestors*, because it offers examples of documentation. Familiarity with the various materials before sitting in the archives is extremely useful, and Hawkings' book has been updated after the first printing of 1992.

CASE STUDIES
Prison
The Chartists in Northallerton
The Chartists wanted electoral reform and mainly worked for votes for working men, along with the reform or electoral districts. In the years around 1840, the 'Physical Force' arm of that movement was accelerating and the Sheffield men were out to take extreme measures. William Martin was given a sentence of one year at Northallerton and he became such a problem that the issue reached Parliament. His charge was seditious language and his behaviour in court tells us a great deal about the man: *The Times* reported:

> On sentence being passed, he struck his hand on the front of the dock, saying, 'Well that will produce a revolution, if anything will.' He begged his Lordship not to send him to Northallerton, but to let him remain in the castle at York, saying that he was very comfortable, and having been seven months confined already was quite at home.

That was a certain way to open up the Northallerton sojourn, as the judges came down hard on Chartists and they would have had no consideration for the radicals' comfort. To Northallerton Martin went, and there he was to stir things up. In court he had already stressed his Irish connections and made reference to Irish issues: he entered into 'a long harangue' on Orangemen, the King of Hanover and Rathcormac'.

Martin refused to work on the treadmill as he had not been sentenced to hard labour and so such a punishment did not fall into that category. He was put into the refractory cell for that refusal, but his case was supported by the Secretary of State, Lord Normanby, who wrote that ' … the prisoner, who was not sentenced to hard labour, cannot legally be placed upon the wheel against his consent… and that if he should refuse to labour upon the wheel, it would be illegal for the gaoler to place him in solitary confinement.' But a visiting magistrate argued against this by quoting one of Peel's recent Gaol Acts which allowed for the work done on a treadmill to be defined as either hard labour or as 'employment for those who are required by law to work for their maintenance...'

Martin, as far as we know, was compelled to work on the mill, and he claimed savage treatment at the hands of the Northallerton staff:

> One morning as soon as I had left my cell, the Governor's son... took me by the collar and dragged me from the place where I stood and threw me with violence against the wall, and on the following day he told me I must expect different treatment from what I received in York and he added that men had been reduced to mere skeletons when their term of imprisonment expired and that it should be the case with me...

These local problems in the treatment of prisoners who had committed 'political' crimes such as sedition, libel or even breaches of the Combination Acts or been involved in illegal trade unions, were the same everywhere. Beverley's house of correction had exactly the same issues with their Chartist, Peddie, from Bradford. But leaving politics aside, the fact was that many of these agitators were involved in firearms and some had every intention of pointing their guns at police constables: some pulled the triggers.

Destination – the asylum

In February 1923, Mrs Grace Castle put her three children in the bath at her Market Place home, Driffield. As if possessed and driven by an inner voice, she forced their heads under the water and drowned them. Three children, the oldest only seven, were found just before midnight that night when police arrived. It has to have been one of the most tragic events in the chronicles of Yorkshire murder. In fact, the very word murder it paradoxically unfitting. Poor Grace Castle was in need of help; her mind was deranged and she had allowed a terrible voice of unreason and destruction to creep into her being.

On that horrendous evening, she had tried to ring her husband Fred, who was at a Freemasons' meeting. But there had been no telephone there. Circumstances conspired that evening to lead the woman to kill. Her husband was a good man, and had fought in the

Great War, coming home to work as a brewer's manager at Market Place. He had also been a well-known local footballer, playing for Driffield and for Cranswick. Not only did she kill her sons, bit she tried to take her own life as well, taking a tincture of iodine. She poignant situation here was that in her mind she had killed the family 'for him'.

When the police officer arrived, Grace Castle was sitting in the kitchen in a state of mental turmoil, saying, 'Oh Mr Waind, you don't know why I have done it!' Why she had done it is difficult to explain but her own words were, in a piece she wrote in her notebook:

Whatever happens don't spend a penny on me. I am cursed and so are my children. The only way I was to have saved their souls was to have killed them....Now I cannot see a way out at all. My husband is the best father and a fine man. He worships his children and what a disappointment for him to have seen them grow up in desperation and crime...

An insight into her condition was provided by the maid in the house, Alice Harper, who was with Mrs Castle earlier that evening. She said that the children were put to bed about a quarter to eight, but that when the children were asleep, Grace was in pain. Alice thought she was suffering from her usual neuralgia. But everyone managed to get to bed, and Alice was roused from her sleep at eleven thirty and she saw Grace sitting in the kitchen saying that her head felt funny and then she said, 'Oh my poor bairns!'

At the first meeting of the coroner's inquest, it was a brief affair and was adjourned. Thomas Holtby, the coroner, summed up the feeling at the time when he said that the deaths constituted the 'saddest tragedy' he had come across. The inquest was adjourned until there was medical evidence. The Rev George Storer presided at the funeral of the children. Grace Castle was charged with murder, having malice aforethought, and of course, was guilty of attempted suicide as well.

Then, at the resumed inquest, some medical evidence came from the family doctor, Dr Keith, a man who had fought alongside Fred Castle in the war. He confirmed that Grace had suffered from some kind of nervous condition for six months; Keith had attended on the night of the deaths and there he found that she had presumably taken the iodine simply because it was something 'chemical', as it was hardly the type of substance a person would take if they wanted to die quickly. All she could say was that the doctor would see by her writings why she had done it. She was totally distracted and although aware of what she had done and how she had killed, it was all somehow unreal to her, outside her range of comprehension.

She was detained in Hull gaol awaiting her trial, and at this point the journalists had begun to be annoyingly insensitive and intrusive, so much so that a member of the jury requested that he make a statement on this, saying that he wished to express strong disapproval of the flash-lights and cameras being used. Through modern eyes, there is nothing unusual or unexpected in this, but in 1923, the moral universe was more rigid and especially in the quieter areas in the provinces, a 'big story' in the eyes of a journalist out to make a name for himself was far from that – it was a terrible local sadness.

At York Assizes in March, Dr Howlett, the prison doctor in Hull, was called to give an assessment of Grace's condition. He confirmed what Dr Simpson, the Medical Superintendent of the East Riding, had said, that though she could put into words the sequence of events on that tragic night, she was unable to feel any impression of emotion or meaning from this. Consequently both medical men agreed that she was insane. In fact, Simpson noted that it was a case of 'long-standing insanity'.

Her youngest son, Kenneth, had been only three, and it was noted during the investigation that Grace castle had been 'in a poor state of health' since Kenneth's birth. As clues to why she chose to kill in this way and for the reasons given, we can theorise that partly her reasons were altruistic – thinking that the one she loved would be better for the lack of stress caused by worry about the children, and also that her own problems (depression) would be alleviated. The tincture of opium is an interesting detail, because it bears no relation to any substance used commonly in these contexts: using that has the hallmark of desperation and irrational thought. It also seems highly likely that Grace Castle was suffering from post-natal depression and in the circumstances in which she had to live, little was done to address this. The spirit of the times was to press on regardless. Even with a maid and help around the house, Grace was still under pressure, and it was from a deep well of unhappiness within her.

Grace Castle was therefore unfit to plead and was admitted to Broadmoor on 9 March 1923. The historian Helen Stewart has tried to follow up the future course of the parents' lives but little has emerged. A man who went to the funeral of the children recalled that Fred Castle had been ill in later life, and had remained a Freemason, but as to Grace, we know nothing of her later life and her ultimate fate stays a mystery.

In Driffield cemetery the gravestone can still be seen, giving testimony to one of the most melancholy stories ever told about murders within a family. There it is recorded that Donald, Hubert and Kenneth Castle rest in peace and that their deaths were 'in tragic circumstances'.

Transportation

A typical case would be like that of Charlotte Barnacle, who was convicted of murder, along with her friend. They had put arsenic in the tea of their employer, not intending to kill her but to make a suffer a little. Clearly they were very wrong. But the jury were lenient, and although the judge was sure that they had intended a malicious act, it was agreed that they were not guilty of 'intending to take away life'.

She arrived in Hobart in 1843, and there she married and had a child. But she and her husband absconded and began a new life in mainland Australia, where they were involved in the mining industry in Tarrawingee. She died in 1896, aged seventy-three.

On the journey, Charlotte would have worn clothes of flannel. In 1849, Alexander Kilroy was campaigning for women convicts to be given thicker and stronger shoes, because he reckoned their thin old shoes were a cause of catarrhal illness. There was no clothing available for the children who came on board; they were in rags from start to finish. Later, the Quaker reformer Elizabeth Fry had an impact on conditions for women on the ships; she formed ladies' committees and this meant that each individual made a parcel of gifts to give to each female convict before her ship left port. This parcel contained a hessian apron and a black cloth one, with a cotton cap and a hessian bag; by 1842 women were being given white jackets and checked aprons in their rations.

Provisions were not so bad. Female prisoners had tea and sugar, and later there was preserved meat and potatoes. But the quantities were not great; in 1844 a man called Clarke was trying to increase the

The penitentiary, Port Arthur, Tasmania (Van Dieman's Land). The author

ration of one pound of meat for the whole voyage. But there were four sit-down meals a week on some ships, and the fare included pork, plum pudding and gruel.

Deaths on the voyages were still high. On six ships sailing between 1792 and 1794, five women from 200 died. One problem was the status and nature of the naval surgeon. As Charles Bateson has written:

As with the naval agent, no attempt was made to define the

naval surgeon's powers or to invest him with the requisite authority... His lowly position increased his difficulties with the commissioned officers in command of the guard and with masters.

Their journals often give us insights into what women had to endure, as in this instance of a punishment: 'In all the course of my life I never heard such expressions come from the mouth of a human being. The woman's hands were tied behind her back and she was gagged.' The woman in question, Elizabeth Barber, was left tied like that through the night. The journal also says, 'The damned whores the moment that they got below, fell a fighting amongst one another.'

But aboard a ship called the *Friendship* it was very different. There, the women did the washing and mending for the officers. One officer noted that they were perfectly behaved for the whole voyage.

But generally, if the murderer's destination was a convict ship, then they had escaped the noose and if they could survive the journey, they would have a chance of a decent new life. Often being given a ticket of leave after five years of good behaviour, meant that they could go into domestic service or farm work outside the prison colony.

Chapter 10

A SURVEY OF SOURCES AND RECORDS

INTRODUCTION
It is clear from all the surveys so far undertaken on sources and support available to the family history researcher that The National Archives are the central, fundamental resource bank. But all family history is subject to a multiplicity of materials, often emerging from any number of offshoots from the central line of enquiry. There is also the logical process of seeing how one criminal or legal action leads to some other, often unexpected, location for the creation of paper records. There has been a proliferation of publications recently, listing and describing all kinds of sources for local an family history, some unexpected and some obvious but often overlooked. My own experience, for instance, has show how undervalued are the contributions from the special interest societies, such as the Surtees Society or the local and regional record societies, whose publications offer sidelights on history and a mass of fascinating primary sources. A typical example of this is the printed production of quarter sessions by various organisations.

For these reasons, what follows is an alphabetical list of some of these other sources. Some are organisations and some are general publications whose importance needs more space here than a mere bibliographical listing. Criminal history has many enthusiasts, from keepers of statistics to small businesses offering little-known information on the past.

ALPHABETICAL LIST
Access to Archives (A2A)
This is a major research database with a catalogue opening up ten million entries from county record offices and other organisations. The real value of this is that it enables the researcher to see what is

available before going to the archive and looking closer at the index.

Annual Register

This extremely valuable resource began publication in 1758 and has been published annually ever since. The purpose was expressed in the first volume by Edmund Burke: 'Not confined to a monthly publication, we have an opportunity of examining with care the products of the year, and selecting what many appear most deserving of notice.' The earlier volumes, up to the mid nineteenth century, have a section called 'Chronicle' and this contains monthly accounts of crimes. There is a close account of each major trial in every year, and church courts as well as the main criminal courts are covered. For instance, this is an extract from one report from 1821 – eight years before the first professional police force when the beadle was at work, but here, the beadle was the offender:

DISTURBANCE IN THE NEW CATHOLIC CHAPEL. The beadle of the new Roman Catholic chapel in Moorfields was summoned before the Lord Mayor on the complaint of a person name Bromley, on a charge of having committed an assault upon him during the performance of the service. Mr Bromley stated that on the afternoon of the Sunday last, he went with his child to see the new Roman Catholic chapel. On entering the door he was beset by persons with plates, who demanded a contribution. He refused to give anything … A Mr Bromley stated that on the afternoon of the Sunday last, he went with his child to see the new Roman Catholic chapel. On entering the door he was beset by persons with plates, who demanded a contribution. He refused to give anything … A person came up to him, intimidating, and demanded threepence and said the complainant had the choice of going out if he did not comply…

The beadle's fate was to be taken into custody and to appear at the next quarter sessions.

Bank of England

As referred to in Chapter 6, the Bank of England records provide sources for forgery cases. Details are online at www.bankofengland .co.uk/about/history/archive/index.htm and David Hawking's article in *Family Tree Magazine* for August 2007 summarises these records. The most enlightening part of these, with regard to the criminal justice system at the time, is arguably the human element in the letters of petition. For instance, in 1820 Martha Lucas had been sentenced to death and she wrote a note from her cell in Newgate, saying, 'I hope you will pardon the liberty I presume in soliciting your kind enterference in behalf of me who is verry much distressed in consequence of my mother being in Betholmoly hospital for some time and my Dear Child is in Great Distress...' (Spellings as per original). This is a good example of the kind of unexpectedly very productive resource which may be easily overlooked and which repays attention, giving a rich perspective on the lives of criminals in times past.

Black Sheep Index
This is a truly fascinating and valuable resource. The site lists criminals as featured in press reports, mostly in the nineteenth century, so the resource is vast and gives a really worthwhile first step if your ancestor was mentioned the newspapers in any way. For instance, this is a typical entry:
Campbell, Bridget maid New Norfolk and Tasmania 1837.
The historian knows at a glance the basic details of transportation and can follow the lead. In addition, for a small fee, the press text can be ordered.

Borthwick Institute for Archives
A new purose-built centre, located adjacent to the J B Morrell Library at the University of York, the Borthwick is an invaluable resource for anyone with criminal ancestors whose cases (or causes) were heard in church courts. Their online catalogue lists several pages of dated material on the various courts: High Commission Court, Archbishop's Court, court books, chancery and audience and citation books. From the 1417 to 1956, these references lead one into specific hearings. Within the cause papers, there are depositions, definitive sentences, libels and allegations. Two volumes of catalogues have been produced: D M Smith's *Ecclesiastical Cause Papers at York: The Court of York 1301-1399* and W J Sheils, *Ecclesiastical Cause Papers at York: Files Transmitted on Appeal 1500-1883*. Both are published by the Institute.

British Association for Local History
Their website is included in the bibliography, but it has to be said that their journal offers in-depth analysis of all kinds of crime and law. There have been lengthy articles on church courts and on county police, for example, in recent years.

Chadwyck-Healey Database
The Chadwyck-Healey Database contains the massive British Trials, 1660-1900. This has first-hand accounts of thousands of trials and records of actual transcripts. There are nine indexes and an 'easy search' to any topic or period. The advertising material says: 'British Trials 1660-1900 republishes… those accounts which were originally published as separate pamphlets or books for sale to the public at large. The majority are verbatim transcripts of what was said in court, and from 1750 these were compiled by the foremost shorthand experts of the day.'

It is in microfiche format, though not many institutions have subscribed at present.

Chetham Society
As with the Surtees Society, but with a focus on Lancashire, the Chetham Society has been producing publications since the 1840s, and has published on such topics in crime history as court leets. The court leet book for Elizabethan Manchester, for instance, has many names included and an index, with accounts of all kinds of petty session dealings.

Crime Writing Chronicles
In 1829, Leman Rede published *York Castle*. This was a chronicle of trials at York assizes over the previous forty years. It was one of a genre of 'true crime' works popular throughout the eighteenth century and regency period, on criminal lives, with accounts of the crime, the capture, the trial, sentence and destinations, together with a moral and religious mini-essay as a coda to each tale, dwelling on the nature of sin and repentance. Names of criminals are there, with witnesses, victims and crime locations. The classic work of the genre is *The Newgate Calendar*, first published in 1773 in five volumes. But the format was copied over the ensuing decades and in 1809 appeared the equally dramatic but informative Criminal Chronology by

Charles Dickens' Household
Narrative, a good source of
contemporary crime.
Author's collection

Andrew Knapp and William Baldwin. The period covered by the
Newgate Calendars was c.1700 to around 1820.

Digital Archives

As mentioned in the text in various chapters, *The Times* and The
Guardian digital archives, together with the British Library's
collections of nineteenth and eighteenth century newspapers and
periodicals, provide a unique access to thousands of criminal and
legal materials. The criminal court structure is more meaningfully
absorbed by using these, because all law reports define the context,
and give the name and location of all trials, whether it is a petty
session or the House of Lords. For instance, this extract from The
Times archive shows these features:

YORK, Friday, July 22 (1825). Criminal court – before Mr Baron Hullock. Isaac Charlesworth was put to the bar, charged with having feloniously and violently stolen and carried away from one Joshua Cropper at Halifax, a £1 note, 14s in silver, a hat and various articles, his property.

The man was sentenced to hang and the sentence was carried out. But that account of the crime, covering perhaps 500 words in *The Times*, opens up a tranche of further historical enquiry (the HO47 judges' reports at TNA for instance, would log any petitions and comments from Hullock himself).

Galleries of Justice

The Galleries of Justice are based in Nottingham, and they have archives on prisons, reformatories, police history, executioners and probation. For family historians, the most valuable part of the collection is the HM Prison Service Archive, as this contains such items as correspondence, transportation letters and remissions from several English prisons. But there is also an archive relating to the London Police Court Mission, with annual reports, minute books and photographs. There are items from reform schools also, and the Associated Societies for the Protection of Women and Children.

History Workshop

This historical journal presents a very useful holding of back issues, many scholars dealing with specific explanations of law, crime, courts and people caught up in the legal process. A typical example is *An Angry and Malicious Mind? Narratives of Slander in the Church Courts of York c. 1660-1760* by Fay Bound.

Household Narrative

Charles Dickens edited this, a companion to *Household Words*. In the 1850s, this periodical recorded a great deal of both London and provincial crime and reported at length on offences such as libel cases, public disorder, murder, assaults and suicides.

Ireland and Irish Sources

There is a wealth of web-based material now to help in the search for Irish criminal ancestors. For a first newspaper search (free) look at

Irish Newspaper Archives at www.Irishnewsarchive.com and then check Irish Roots, Irish Family Research and Irish Abroad sites (listed in my Bibliography).

Journals
For the social history and the context of crimes, see the specialist studies often in *BBC History Magazine* (a recent issue focused on forgery); *Past and Present; Social History and Social and Cultural History* (see Bibliography).

London Metropolitan Archives
The LMA has court records from 1549 of the City, Middlesex and Westminster Sessions of the Peace, magistrates' courts and some coroners' inquests for City, London and Middlesex. There are also diocesan records, so the Diocese of London Consistory Court records are there. There are some transportation records also, a separate series of papers with bonds of shipmasters – those contracted to carry convicts – and copy orders to keepers of prisons. There are bonds for 1682, 1720-1787 at MJ/SPT and ACC/1268 and returns of expenses for 1837 and 1856-57 at MJ/SPT. There are lists of convicts waiting to be transported from 1782-1790 at MA/G/GEN/1126-1185.

Memoirs and autobiographies
As with all varieties of historical study, the primary sources are the ones closest to the events, and although they may be very subjective and biased, their factual basis and human perspectives on what is often merely a documentary topic is extremely useful. Prisoner memoirs have become a literary genre of their own, with lots of contemporary observation and comment. Typical of this is Samuel Bamford's *Passages in the Life of a Radical* (1843) which gives several accounts of life as a prisoner at the time for a working man with a radical cast of mind and a militant nature. He even has a detailed account of the last days of two men condemned to die at Lincoln Castle and gives a first-hand account of an execution.

Arguably the best collection of these texts used in a survey of prison history is *Victorian Prison Lives* by Philip Priestley (Pimlico, 1999) which makes use of dozens of prison writings. Similar books on prison history, with narratives of specific prisoners have appeared recently, including *The Gaol*, the history of Newgate, by Kelly Grovier (John Murray, 2008).

Old Bailey Sessions

The online Old Bailey sessions include transcripts of 210,000 trials held here, at the Central Criminal Court, between 1674 and 1913. The trails records include a large amount of biographical information, and of course, as there are around 3,000 records of executions, there is a fair chance that your 'Black Sheep' ended his life at Tyburn. We owe this facility to the Humanities Research Institute, the University of Sheffield and the Open University. A recent feature on the site reported that 'Researcher Joan Brewer found her husband's great-great-grandmother, Phoebe Douglas, who was transported to Australia in 1829.'

The National Archives

TNA has lots to offer, but perhaps most useful in this context are the information leaflets, explaining such topics as assize records, but is also very useful for help with questions of immigration and adoption in family history research.

Scottish Legal System

If this is your concern, then use www.nas.gov.uk/guides/default.asp. The Scottish criminal legal system has different terms, functions and processes to that of England. For a clear, concise explanation see 'Law and Disorder' by Sheena Tait in the May 2007 issue of *Family Tree Magazine* pp. 24-27. This is a very readable explanation of the court system.

Skeleton in the Cupboard

This is a regular feature in *Your Family Tree* magazine. Every month, a reader writes a piece on the search for a criminal ancestor. A recent issue involved an account of a juvenile offence tracing the fate of an ancestor who was 'banged up overnight and birched' for a minor offence in 1880. Other publications have similar features, and one of the most informative aspects of this is that the stories reveal the nature of crimes at times in the past, in comparison with their status (or absence) in the criminal justice system today.

Smugglers' Britain

There has been no specific mention of smugglers in the foregoing pages, but this web site helps here. This is www.smuggling.co

.uk/trace.html and it offers links to TNA, but also to indexes for convicts and ticket-of-leave sources. For instance, there is the Tasmanian Name Index – and Tasmania was the site of Port Arthur, one of the main convict pentitentiaries in Australia.

Suffragettes' Records

At the section 'Your Archives' at TNA there is material of suffragette prisoners. During the campaign for the votes for women movement in Edwardian Britain, the militants were, naturally, criminals, and served terms in gaol. Much of this documentation has been the basis of recent books, but if your ancestor was a suffragette and was in custody, then this is the place to look. The main TNA references are: Cabinet Office, CAB series 41, with letters and reports; Home Office, HO45 series with such things as letters of complaint from prisoners; HO 144 series and the Metropolitan Police series MEPO 2, which includes material both famous and little-known suffragettes.

Surtees Society

The Surtees Society publications cover a variety of criminal history works, including justicing notebooks and quarter sessions records. It was founded in 1834 by Robert Surtees, a Durham historian. For family researchers in the North East, this is worth a look. A typical publication in this context is Durham Quarter Sessions Rolls for 1471-1625.

Ticket of Leave Book – Sheffield Archives

This item is typical of the wealth of extra, surprisingly useful information often found in provincial records. In the case of Sheffield, this is a list of names in the Ticket of Leave Book for 1864-1874 and gives name, age, origin, date of conviction, place of conviction and occupation. This was compiled with the help of Sheffield and District Family History Society.

When a Case does not Reach a Court?

Finally, there is the thrill for the historian of sheer serendipity: something 'turns up' unexpectedly. Chris Brooke reported on a case, writing in the *Daily Mail* in December 2008 on a Victorian case that would have been before a magistrate for bastardy and paternal affiliation had it not been for some 'buying silence'. A document was found in some archives in Rotherham which reveals this story. The document is a signed statement by both parties involved agreeing that the true identity of Herbert Higginbotham would never be revealed; that was in 1874 and only now is the truth known. The wealthy son of businessman George Haywood, one William, had an affair with the daughter of an employee – George Higginbotham. The cost of his silence was, in modern values, £50,000.

The interest here for the family and crime historian is that the document represents the kind of material that prevented a legal process and a prosecution. The archivist concerned said, 'It is quite unusual to find this kind of private arrangement for the care of an illegitimate child. Generally you would only get this information if the matter had gone to a magistrates' court to obtain a maintenance order.'

Elizabeth Higginbotham later moved to London and there she could have a fresh start in life; William died in 1918.

Reporting in the mid-Victorian years. Author's collection

AFTERWORD

THE PROCESS OF RESEARCH

The first discovery: an ancestor is missing from a census perhaps, or you follow up a snippet of information from the family oral history. Note any details you know from any sources at all. These may well be inaccurate. A recent question to a true crime magazine asked about a murder that took place in Doncaster 'some time between about 1960 and 1980'. The offence may not be known, so the next step is a trawl through court records.

Go to the large databases and search for the name within the time-span the offence took place. The Times Digital Archive will provide most court reports, and if a report is found, that sentence will lead you to the next stage. Another very useful step at this stage is to consult the Black Sheep Index and search for your named offender. That could lead you to the press report or anything in the press about him or her.

From the sentence of the court in question, the destination will be one of these (a) acquittal (b) prison sentence at home (c) transportation or (d) execution.

All other materials will expand this bare outline. For instance, if the criminal went to gaol, you have all the categories of prison records to look at. The police records will confirm all this, so in total the options are:
- Calendar of prisoners
- Prison registers
- Any other prison records such as surgeons' reports
- Police charge books
- Station record books

The social history will then build on this. All report details reach out to other aspects of life such as poverty, unemployment, mental illness etc and these of course have their documentation.

Write a biography, incorporating all of this, with the larger topics integrated into the criminal trajectory from crime to sentence.

The nature of the offence and the time it was committed are the determining factors of course. For instance, this summary shows some contrasts:

Summary offence – magistrates' court or a petty session/police court – short prison sentence in a local gaol.

Indictable offence - magistrates' court – assize court – trial records – sentence – court of appeal (after 1907) – possibly a higher court such as King's Bench or any other criminal superior court (treason, sedition, mutiny etc.). Remember that the assizes ended in 1971 and from that point were replaced by crown courts.

A scene from Newgate. Author's collection

Offence in non-criminal court such as a church court or an earlier manorial or leet court before c.1700 – trial – cause heard – decision of fine or deprivation/dismissal etc.

With early assize rolls, medieval period, the assize was either heard by county justices (the sheriff) or by the travelling justices at the assize twice a year.

For debt, insolvency, bankruptcy – civil courts are the place to look, so the assizes had a 'crown side' for that as well as the 'criminal side'.

Finally, for military offences: the process would overlap but your search would have to include:
• Admiralty courts
• Courts martial
• Military records – central and regimental

An interesting sidelight on this is the duel. Duelling was illegal from the early nineteenth century but often duels between officers would take place and the hearing might be in a military court rather than in a criminal court, even if there had been a homicide.

So overall, the process of law is offence-arrest-indictment-trail-conviction

BIBLIOGRAPHY AND RESOURCES

Books

I have organised this according to categories of books and sources, using and sometimes describing how these relate to criminal history. Most are in print but some extremely useful works in this area are out of print; if that is the case, I have selected only those volumes which are without question especially useful in the search for criminal ancestors.

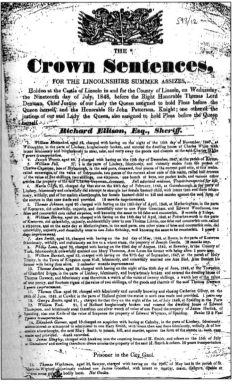

A document showing Crown Sentences. Lincolnshire Archives

A Note on Primary Printed Sources
Throughout the book, there have been references to classic works of crime narrative, and also to some hard-to-find texts such as autobiographies and biographies of criminals. Much of this is accessible online through the Old Bailey sessions records, but these may be worthwhile also:
The Newgate Calendar (Various editions). Typical of these is the Folio edition, with old engravings, edited by Sir Norman Birkett in 1951.
Philip Priestley's *Victorian Prison Lives* (Pimlico, 1999) uses a large number of memoirs in order to reconstruct the daily lives of people in gaol in that period. Other useful biographical material on the lives of judges, lawyers, prisoners and criminals are:
Bamford, Samuel, *Passages in the Life of a Radical* (Oxford, 1984).
Douglas, Robert, *At Her Majesty's Pleasure* (Hodder, 2007).
Humphreys, Sir Travers, *A Book of Trials* (Pan, 1953).
Humphreys, Sir Travers, *Criminal Days* (Hodder and Stoughton, 1945).

Reference – General Crime History and Family History
The *Annual Register* – from the early eighteenth century, still in existence, but for full crime reports and trials reports, the numbers up to the mid nineteenth centuries are the most useful.
Cyriax, Oliver, *The Penguin Encyclopaedia of Crime* (Penguin, 1993.
Hawkings, David T, *Criminal Ancestors. A guide to historical criminal records in England and Wales* (Sutton, 1992).
Paley, Ruth and Fowler, Simon, *Family Skeletons* (The National Archives, 2005).
Pearsall, Mark, *The National Archives Family History Companion* (TNA, 2007).

Family History
Bell, Gail, *The Poison Principle* – a memoir of family secrets and literary poisoning (Pan Books, 2002).
Blatchford, Robert & Elizabeth (Eds.) *The Family and Local History Handbook* (Robert Blatchford in association with *Family History Monthly* and *Family Tree/Practical Family History Magazine*, published 1997-2009, currently 12 volumes). This provides an excellent compendium of articles on all aspects of the subject. As well as an archive reference section, featuring police records and others, there are always features on criminal history in each volume.

Busby, Sian, *The Cruel Mother* (Short Books, 2004). This is a family memoir combined with a research project based on Sian's great-grandmother who was sentenced to an indefinite term in Broadmoor in 1919.

Chater, Kathy, *How to Trace Your Family Tree* (Hermes House, 2003).

Fowler, Simon (Ed.), *Starting Out in Family History* (TNA 2008).

Iredale, David and Barrett, John, *Discovering Your Family Tree* (Shire, 2002). This is particularly useful on justices of the peace and on the courts.

Landale, James, *Duel – a true story of death and honour* (Canongate, 2005). In 1826 a businessman, David Landale, shot his bank manager dead in a duel. The author delves into Scottish family history to follow the trail; David Landale was found not guilty.

Local History

Carter, Paul and Thompson, Kate, *Sources for Local Historians* (Phillimore, 2005). This is excellent on information regarding assize courts and police. It is also arguably the best book for the reproduction of documents of all kinds.

Friar, Stephen, *The Sutton Companion to Local History* (Sutton, 2001).

Richardson, John, *The Local Historian's Encyclopaedia*, (Historical Publications, 1974). Although this is out of print, it is worth tracing because it has sections arranged alphabetically, including a Law and Order section and other related sections such as welfare, militia etc.

Social History/History of Crime and Law

Arieno, Marlene, *Victorian Lunatics: a social epidemiology of mental illness in mid-nineteenth century England* (Susquehanna University Press, 1989).

Barnard, Sylvia M, *Viewing the Breathless Corpse. Coroners and inquests in Victorian Leeds* (Words@Woodmere, 2001).

Birkenhead, The Earl of, *Famous Trials* (Hutchinson, 1925). This has accounts of several high-profile trials, covering treason, murder, fraud and sedition.

Cobley, John, *The Crimes of the First Fleet Convicts* (Sydney, 1970).

Cook, Chris, *Britain in the Nineteenth Century 1815-1914* (Routledge, 2005).

Cowie, L W, *The Wordsworth Dictionary of Social History* (Wordsworth, 1996).

Denning, Lord, *Landmarks in the Law* (Butterworths, 1984).

Emsley, Clive, *Crime and Society in England 1750-1900*, (Longman, 1987).

Gregory, Jeremy and Stevenson, John, *Britain in the Eighteenth Century* (Routledge, 2007).

Hibbert, Christopher, *The Roots of Evil. A social history of crime and punishment* (Sutton, 2003).

Hughes, Robert, *The Fatal Shore*, (Collins Harvill, 1987).

Jackson, Lee, *A Dictionary of Victorian London*, (Anthem, 2006).

McKie, David, *Jabez. The Rise and Fall of a Victorian Rogue* (Atlantic Books, 2004).

Morgan, Gwenda and Rushton, Peter, *Eighteenth Century Criminal Transportation* (Palgrave, 2004).

Morris, Norval and Rothman, David J, *The Oxford History of the Prison* (Oxford, 1998).

Naphy, William, *Sex Crimes from Renaissance to Enlightenment*, (Tempus, 2002)

Nicholl, Charles, *The Lodger*, (Penguin, 2007).

Osborne, Bertram, *Justices of the Peace 1361-1848* (Oxford, 1977).

Porter, Bernard, *Plots and Paranoia – a history of political espionage in Britain* (Routledge, 1989). This is excellent for the crime of sedition in the Regency period and for treason in later times.

Rees, Sian, *The Floating Brothel* (Headline, 2001).

Saul, Nigel, *A Companion to Medieval England 1066-1485* (Tempus, 2005).

Sharpe, J A, *Crime in Early Modern England 1550-1750* (Longman, 1984).

Summers, Ann, *Damned Whores and God's Police* (Melbourne, 1982).

[Editor's note: Most book titles listed as 'Sutton' and 'Tempus' are now under the ownership of The History Press.]

Newspapers, Journals and Periodicals
General
For newspaper reports of crimes and trials, The Times Digital Archive and The Guardian Digital Archive are well worth the effort and expense of subscription. Some public libraries may provide free access, so it is worth checking. In addition there is the online facility of the British Library's Nineteenth Century British Newspapers/

Periodicals search process.

These periodicals are worth looking at for features on all aspects of crime and law in their period:

Daily Graphic (this has police court features and reports from other courts)
Gentleman's Magazine
Household Narrative (for the 1850s and 1860s)
Illustrated London News
Strand Magazine (1890s in particular)

Specific articles on crimes and criminal law

Academic journals often have excellent features on the social context of crime, at all stages in history, so the indexes of social history journals are always worth searching, and the case is the same for journals of criminology or the Prison Service.

Ancestors magazine, issue 17, Dec 2003: special issue of crime and punishment.
This has features on quarter sessions, justices of the peace and a transportation case study.

Heather, Chris 'Licences at Large' in *Ancestors* magazine, issue 74, Oct 2008.
This is a special feature on the newly accessible database at TNA on female prisoners.

Keneally, Thomas, 'Convict Nation' in *BBC History Magazine*, July, 2006 pp. 35-40.

Kesselring, Krista, 'Detecting Death Disguised' in *History Today*, April, 2006 pp. 20-26.
This explains issues related to early coroners' courts.

King, Peter, 'The Summary Courts and Social Relations in Eighteenth Century England', in *Past and Present*, May 2004, No.183, pp.125-172. This is a very comprehensive survey of the smaller courts and how they worked.

Thomas, Jenny, 'Tracing Your Criminal Ancestors' in *Who Do You Think You Are* magazine, BBC, issue 3, Dec 2007.

Websites

These listings are sites with material on criminal records and on related social historical subjects which prove valuable in research in this area. The major general sites are mostly not included.

Access to Archives www.a2a.org.uk
Archives Hub www.archiveshub.ac.uk
Archives Network Wales www.archivesnetworkwales.info
Australian Family History Compendium www.cohsoft.com.au/afhc
Australian national Archives www.naa.gov.au
BBC Family History www.bbc.co.uk/history/familyhistory
Blacksheep Ancestors www.Blacksheepancestors.com
The Borthwick Institute www.york.ac.uk/inst/bihr
British History Online www.british-history.ac.uk
British Library www.bl.uk/familyhistory.html
Cemeteries of Australia www.ozgenonline.com/aust_ cemeteries
Chartist Ancestors www.Chartists.net
Clergy of the Church of England Database www.theclergydatabase.
  org.uk
Convict Records in Australia www. Coraweb.com.au/convict.html
Federation of Family History Societies www.ffhs.org.uk
The Genealogist www.thegenealogist.co.uk
Guardian and Observer Digital Archive archive-guardian.co.uk
Irish Abroad www.irishabroad.com/yourroots
Irish Newspaper Archives www.irishnewsarchive.com
Lambeth Palace Library www.lambethpalacelibrary.org
London Generations www.cityoflondon.gov.uk/londonGenerations
Medieval English Genealogy www.medievalgenealogy.org.uk
Metropolitan Police History www.met.police.uk/history
The National Archives www.nationalarchives.go.uk
National Archives of Scotland www.nas.gov.uk
National Library of Wales www.llgc'org.uk
Old Bailey Trials www.oldbaileyonline.org
Scotland's people www.scotland'speople.gov.uk
Trade Union Ancestors www.unionancestors.co.uk
Victorian Web www.Victorianweb.org.
A Web of English History www.historyhome.co.uk
Workhouses www.workhouses.org.

A FINAL NOTE AND A
SEARCH STILL ONGOING

Other sources may well come from family history society sites and chat rooms. There are always question and answer pages in the family history magazines and a host of enthusiastic history groups who will each have their own records and sources. In my own research, I was looking at the Billingtons, a dynasty of hangmen, very prominent in British criminal history, and a family history site proved to be invaluable in that hunt for biographical information. Equally, the great web of knowledge that historians enjoy having to explore and hopefully find hidden treasures, goes on and on being enlarged. Often in the most obscure memoirs, the historian finds a witness to an event the ancestor was involved in, and the material grows yet again.

A search for a criminal ancestor by an American researcher is still going on, at the time of writing frustrated by gaps in the corpus of source material, but the detective work goes on. This particular story concerns a certain Thomas Killaley, whose family came to England from Ireland as so many did, in the early nineteenth century and then settled at first in Manchester and then split as one brother settled in Bole, North Nottinghamshire. His family, the Killelays who worked in reed-making by the river Trent, are listed in the East Retford records of the 1871 census, appear to lead to no criminality.

Thomas is a different matter. He is listed in the 1881 census, married to Mary, living at Ancoats in Manchester in the ward of New Cross. This Thomas was part of the more politically active Killelays and there are references showing that they had the 'ribbon man' militancy. These were men of a secret society, taking oaths and being subversive against the British authority. Thomas was in fact linked to the Fenians. After the notorious Fenian outrage of 1865 when a police sergeant in Manchester was killed while escorting prisoners, it seems that Thomas was one of the lesser echelons of that movement. He was imprisoned in Dartmoor a political prisoner, and is listed there in the returns of prisoners in 1891. Therefore some time around the age of thirty, he was involved in a militant action and arrested.

Such are the frustrations of this research that nothing else can be ascertained about his time in Dartmoor or his release. The records for that period there are not available. He had had one earlier spell in gaol and was released in 1878 but then was in trouble again. That is all that is known so far, but the search goes on. It has to be said that the researcher cannot actually go to records in Ireland at the moment. Consequently this illustrates the limits of what may be found when merely keeping to online sources. A point comes at which visits to archives have to be made to complete the story.

GLOSSARY

This is a basic list of legal terms which tend to occur in the research process involved in finding a family 'black sheep'. Most are mentioned in my text.

Assize courts	The various assizes on the circuits in England and Wales at which the judges would hear cases twice a year – these were felonies, more serious, indictable crimes.
calendar of prisoners	This is a document showing all essential information on convicted people: name, age, magistrate, date of custody, offence, detailsof the trail and sentence.
Criminal register	This document gives details of convicts: repeating calendarinformation.
deposition	This was an examination of the defendant and the witnesses.
felony	offences were formerly defined in the common law as felonies misdemeanour or misdemeanours. A felony meant the loss of land and goods until the Forfeiture Act of 1870. A misdemeanour was any offence that did not constitute a felony.
Grand jury	This was conceived at the Assize of Clarendon in 1166; the idea was that this body of an uneven number of men would make a presentment for an indictment relating to a criminal offence. If a drafted bill (indictment) was found to be a 'true bill' then the defendant would have to face a trial by the jury of twelve. If there was a not guilty decision then the bill was

	'ignoramus' – there being no case to answer. The grand jury was abolished in 1948.
House of correction	The name for a local prison or 'bridewell' – both terms used interchangeably in early writings.
indictable	An offence triable since 1971 at Crown Court and formerly at
summary assize	in contrast, a summary offence need not be heard before a jury.
indictment	A formal statement of the charge against the accused person.
King's Bench	The highest criminal court.
Latin in assizes	Before 1733 assize records were in Latin. Later, there were still Latin abbreviations used: *Ca null catalla nulla* – no goods to forfeit. *Cog ind cognovits* indictamentum – confessed to indictment. *Cul culpabilis* - guilty. *Ign ignoramus* - no case to answer. *Non cul nec re* - *non culpabilis nec retraxit* – not guilty and did not flee. *Po se point se super patriam* – puts himself on the country (chooses a Jury trial). *Sus suspendatur* – let him be hanged. *Nisi prius* This was a trial by jury with a single judge, at assizes.
Order books	These were formal records of court proceedings.
Palatinate courts	The counties of Cheshire, Durham and Lancashire were known as Palatinates. Changes were made in 1830 in Cheshire; the Durham court continued until 1876 (then being amalgamated into the North Eastern Assize circuit). Lancashire also had a Palatinate court until 1876. These court records are in The National Archives.
Parish Constable	The official responsible for law and order,

	before the first professional police who gradually appeared, after the Police Act of 1829 which created the Metropolitan Police.
Petitions	In quarter sessions, petitions refer to bills of costs for prosecutions.
Plaintiff	The person prosecuting in court.
Quarter sessions	The trials heard four times a year, run by justices of the peace.
Recognisance	A document binding a witness to appear at court.
Respite	A discharge – in times past, it was the reprieve given to a condemned felon by the Home Secretary.
Superior court	One of the higher level courts dealing with trials of very serious crime; these are both civil and criminal of course.

INDEX